FastCourse

MICROSOFT®

Excel *2007*

LEVEL 1 OF 3

Trisha Hakola

Poway Adult School

LABYRINTH
L E A R N I N G ®

FastCourse Excel 2007: Level 1
by Trisha Hakola

Copyright © 2009 by Labyrinth Learning

Labyrinth Learning
PO Box 20818
El Sobrante, California 94820
800.522.9746
On the web at www.lablearning.com

President:
Brian Favro

Series Editor:
Russel Stolins

Acquisitions Editor:
Jason Favro

Managing Editor:
Laura A. Lionello

Production Manager:
Rad Proctor

Editorial/Production Team:
DocumentJones, Donnali Fifield,
Karen Henry, ITC, and Tess Roach

Indexing: Joanne Sprott

Cover Illustration:
Béatrice Favereau

Cover Design:
Seventeenth Street Studios

ITEM: 1-59136-203-2
ISBN-13: 978-1-59136-203-6

Manufactured in the United States of America.

10 9 8 7 6 5 4 3 2

FastCourse Excel 2007:
Level 1

Table of Contents

LESSON 1

Exploring Excel 2007

In this lesson, you will develop fundamental Excel 2007 skills. This lesson will provide you with a solid understanding of Excel so you are prepared to master the advanced features introduced in later lessons. You will learn how to navigate around a worksheet, enter various types of data, and select cells.

LESSON OBJECTIVES

After studying this lesson, you will be able to:

- Explain ways Excel can help your productivity
- Launch the Excel program
- Navigate around the Excel window
- Utilize the tabs and Ribbon to issue commands
- Enter text and numbers into cells
- Distinguish between a text and a number entry in a cell
- Save and "save as" your workbooks
- Close a workbook and exit from Excel

LESSON TIMING

- Concepts/Hands-On: 1 hr 00 min
- Concepts Review: 15 min
- Total: 1 hr 15 min

CASE STUDY: BUILDING A BASIC SPREADSHEET

Charlie Arnold is a volunteer coordinator at South Coast Hospital. Mendy Laubach, the human resources manager for the hospital, has asked Charlie to maintain a list of hours worked by his volunteers from Wednesday to Sunday (Charlie's workweek). Mendy asks Charlie to report the data on a daily basis. After analyzing Mendy's request, Charlie decides that Excel 2007 is the right tool for the job and proceeds to organize the data in a worksheet.

Presenting Excel 2007

Microsoft Office Excel 2007 is an electronic spreadsheet program. It allows you to work with numbers and data much more efficiently than the pen-and-paper method. Excel is used in virtually all industries and many households for a variety of tasks such as:

- Creating and maintaining detailed budgets

- Keeping track of extensive customer lists

- Performing "what-if" scenarios and break-even analyses

- Determining the profitability of a business or sector

- Creating tables to organize information

- Tracking employee information

- Producing detailed charts to graphically display information

- Creating invoices or purchase orders

- Determining the future value of an investment, the present value of an annuity, or the payment for a loan

- Working with reports exported from small business accounting software programs such as Intuit's QuickBooks®

As you can see from this list, Excel is not just used to crunch numbers. It is a very powerful program that is used not only to work with numbers but also to maintain databases. If you have started a database in Excel, you can even import it into Microsoft Access (the program in the Microsoft Office Suite that is specialized for working with databases). Many people may use Excel to track their databases rather than Access because of its ease of use and because Access is not included in all of the Microsoft Office editions. If you are tracking multiple databases that you wish to include in reports and data queries, you will want to consider utilizing Access, though, as it really is designed to work with multiple tables of data.

Starting Excel

The method you use to start Excel depends in large part on whether you intend to create a new workbook or open an existing workbook. A workbook is a file containing one or more worksheets. To create a new workbook, use one of the following methods. Once the Excel program has started, you can begin working in the new workbook that appears.

- Click the **start** button and choose Microsoft Office Excel 2007 from the All Programs menu. (Depending on your installation of Microsoft Office, you may need to choose Microsoft Office from the All Programs menu and then choose Microsoft Office Excel 2007.)

- Click the Microsoft Office Excel 2007 button on the Quick Launch toolbar located to the right of the Start button. (This button may not appear on all computers.)

Use one of the following methods if you intend to open an existing Excel workbook. Once the Excel program has started, the desired workbook will open in an Excel window.

■ Navigate to the desired document using Windows Explorer or My Computer and double-click the workbook.

■ Click the button and point to My Recent Documents. You can choose the desired workbooks from the documents list, which displays the most-recently used documents.

Hands-On 1.1   Start Excel

1. Start your computer, and the Windows Desktop will appear.

2. Click the button and choose (All) Programs.

3. Choose the Microsoft Office folder, and then choose Microsoft Office Excel 2007.

Exploring the Excel Program Window

When you launch Excel, you will see a blank workbook displayed. The window is filled with many objects and a space for you to create your spreadsheet. Using the figures that follow, you will have an opportunity to learn the names of some of the objects that you can see on your screen.

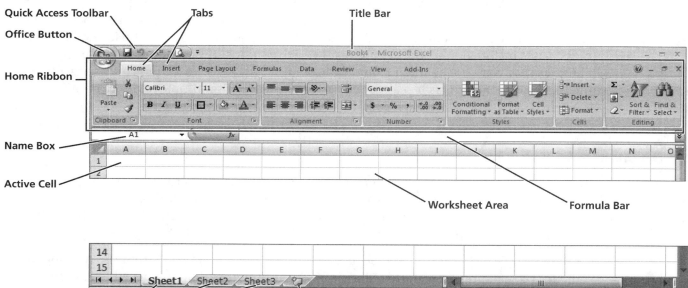

Using Worksheets and Workbooks

Excel displays a blank workbook the moment you start the program. A workbook is composed of worksheets. This is similar to a paper notebook with many sheets of paper. You enter text, numbers, formulas, charts, and other objects in worksheets. By default, Excel displays three worksheets in a new workbook, each accessible by a separate tab at the bottom of the screen. The maximum number of worksheets you can insert is limited only by the amount of memory available on your computer.

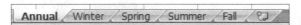

In this example, the sheet tabs are named so that you can organize data for each season as well as track annual information.

A worksheet has a grid structure with horizontal rows and vertical columns. A new worksheet has 16,384 columns and 1,048,576 rows! However, at any given time only a small number of the rows and columns are visible in the worksheet

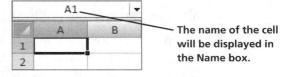

The name of the cell will be displayed in the Name box.

window. The intersection of each row and column is a cell. Each cell is identified by a reference. The reference is the column letter followed by the row number. For example, A1 is the reference of the cell in the top-left corner of the worksheet. So, we refer to this as cell A1.

Mousing Around in Excel

The shape of the mouse pointer will change as you move it around the Excel window. The shape of the pointer will let you know what will happen if you click over that spot.

Mouse Pointer Shape	Function
✚	Click to select a cell.
	Click and drag to select multiple cells.
✛	The fill handle pointer; you will learn what this tool can do for you in Lesson 2, Editing, Viewing, and Printing Worksheets.
▨	Allows you to perform a variety of tasks when clicked, such as issue a command from the Ribbon or select a new tab.
✛	The move pointer; if you drag with this, it will move cell contents from one location to another.
↔	The resize pointer; dragging this pointer will allow you to change the size of objects such as rows, pictures, and charts.
→ ↓	Select a row or column.
I	Click with the I-beam pointer to enter text, such as in the Formula Bar.

Scrolling Along in a Worksheet

There are two scroll bars visible in the Excel window, both vertical and horizontal. They allow you to see other areas of the worksheet without changing which cell is active. There are three ways to use the scroll bars to view other areas of your spreadsheet.

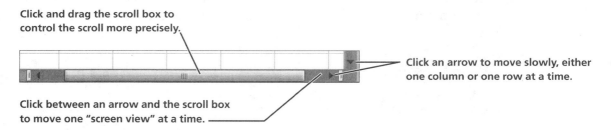

Click and drag the scroll box to control the scroll more precisely.

Click an arrow to move slowly, either one column or one row at a time.

Click between an arrow and the scroll box to move one "screen view" at a time.

Navigating in a Worksheet

When you have a cell selected, it is surrounded by a thick line, which indicates that it is the active cell. You can change the active cell by clicking in another cell or by using the keyboard. This is important because data is entered into the active cell. The vertical and horizontal scroll bars let you navigate through a worksheet; however, scrolling does not change which cell is active. After scrolling you will have to select which cell is to be active, either by clicking or using one of the keystrokes listed below.

Keystroke(s)	How the Highlight Moves
→ ← ↑ ↓	One cell right, left, up, or down
Home	Beginning of current row
Ctrl + →	End of current row
Ctrl + Home	Home cell, usually cell A1
Ctrl + End	Last cell in active part of worksheet
Page Down	Down one visible screen
Page Up	Up one visible screen
Alt + Page Down	One visible screen right
Alt + Page Up	One visible screen left
Ctrl + G	Displays Go To dialog box—enter cell reference and click OK

 Hands-On 1.2   Move the Selection and Explore the Excel Window

1. Slide the mouse over the screen and notice the thick cross shape ✚ when it is in the worksheet area.

2. Click the cross-shaped pointer on any cell and notice that the cell becomes active.

3. Move the selection five times by clicking in various cells.

4. Use the →, ←, ↑, and ↓ keys to position the highlight in cell F10.

5. Tap the Home key and see that the highlight moves to cell A10.

6. Press Ctrl + Home to make A1 the active cell.

7. Tap the Page Down key two or three times.

8. Press and hold down the ↑ key until A1 is the active cell.

9. Click the Scroll Right ▶ button on the horizontal scroll bar until columns AA and AB are visible.

10. Click the Scroll Down ▼ button on the vertical scroll bar until row 100 is visible.

11. Take a few minutes to practice scrolling and moving the selection.

12. Press Ctrl + G to display the Go To dialog box.

13. Type **g250** in the Reference box and click OK.

14. Use the Go To command to move to two or three different cells.

15. Press Ctrl + Home to return to cell A1.

16. Follow these steps to explore the Excel window:

Ⓐ Notice the Name box.

Ⓑ Click the Sheet2 tab and notice that a blank worksheet appears. The number of worksheets you can have is limited only by the amount of available memory in the computer.

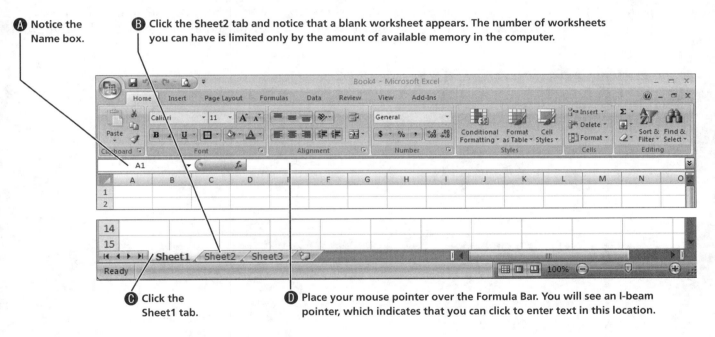

Ⓒ Click the Sheet1 tab.

Ⓓ Place your mouse pointer over the Formula Bar. You will see an I-beam pointer, which indicates that you can click to enter text in this location.

17. Press Ctrl + Home to move the highlight to cell A1.

Working with Tabs and Ribbons

In Microsoft Office 2007, Excel does not have the traditional menu and toolbars with which computer users are familiar. You are able to access the commands that will allow you to effectively utilize Excel through the tabs, ribbons, and Office button located at the top of window.

The Office Button

  The Office button, when clicked, accesses a menu that allows you to issue file management commands. File management simply means working with Excel on the level of the "file"—such as creating new files, opening existing files, saving the file you are working on, and printing your file.

The Quick Access Toolbar

Excel 2007 has one remaining toolbar (compared with previous versions), which is located at the top of the window. It is similar to the Quick Launch toolbar in Windows in that it contains commands that you use frequently. It is also customizable, unlike the Ribbon, which is set. The Quick Access toolbar, with the default buttons, is displayed in the following illustration.

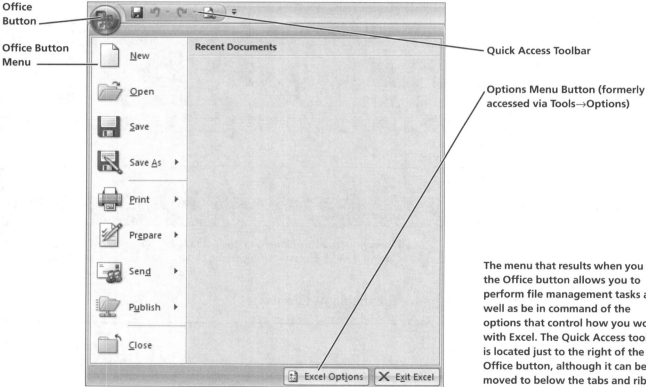

Office Button

Office Button Menu

Quick Access Toolbar

Options Menu Button (formerly accessed via Tools→Options)

The menu that results when you click the Office button allows you to perform file management tasks as well as be in command of the options that control how you work with Excel. The Quick Access toolbar is located just to the right of the Office button, although it can be moved to below the tabs and ribbon.

Customizing the Quick Access Toolbar

The Quick Access toolbar can be customized to include commands that you frequently use. If you regularly use the Open command, you may wish to add it to the Quick Access toolbar, as shown.

Displaying Tabs and Working with Ribbons

The tabs at the top of the Excel window organize the commands into eight categories. The commands appear on ribbons displayed across the screen. In order to view a new tab, you simply need to single-click it. The commands on the Ribbon can be chosen by a single-click as well.

Excel's Home Ribbon

The standard tabs along with the Ribbon are displayed in the preceding illustration. Additional contextual tabs will become visible as necessary. For instance, if you are working with a picture, a picture tab will appear.

The Ribbon with a contextual tab displayed. When a picture is selected, a special Picture Tools Format tab appears. All of the commands on this ribbon deal with the formatting of the picture.

ScreenTips

A ScreenTip is a little window that appears to describe the function of the object at which you are pointing. ScreenTips appear when you rest your mouse pointer over an option on a ribbon, the Quick Access toolbar, or the Office button. In Excel 2007, there are also Enhanced ScreenTips that appear for some of the commands. An Enhanced ScreenTip is a larger window that is more descriptive than a ScreenTip and also provides a link to an Excel help topic.

When you place your mouse pointer over an object on the Ribbon, a ScreenTip appears.

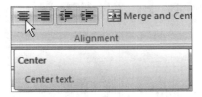

Sometimes you will see an Enhanced ScreenTip when you place your mouse pointer over an object. In this case, you receive an Enhanced ScreenTip explaining the function of the Office button with a link to a help topic.

Dialog Box Launchers

Many of the groups on the Ribbon have Dialog Box Launchers 🖾. Clicking on the dialog box launcher will open a window that allows you to issue additional commands.

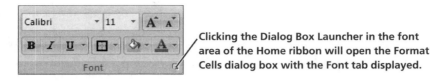

Clicking the Dialog Box Launcher in the font area of the Home ribbon will open the Format Cells dialog box with the Font tab displayed.

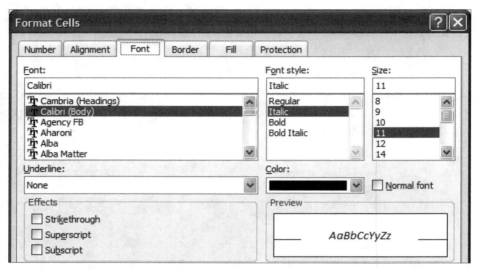

The Font tab of the Format Cells dialog box allows you to make changes to how the font appears in the selected cell(s).

Hiding the Ribbon

There may be times when you do not want the Ribbon displayed at the top of the window. In order to hide it, simply double-click on the tab that is currently displayed. To display the Ribbon once again, click on the tab you wish to view.

 Hands-On 1.3 **Explore the Tabs, Ribbons, and Quick Access Toolbar**

1. Click the Page Layout tab at the top of the window.

2. Click the Dialog Box Launcher at the bottom-right corner of the Page Setup section of the Ribbon.

3. Click the Cancel button at the bottom of the dialog box to close it.

4. Move your mouse pointer over various commands on the Page Layout tab of the Ribbon display their ScreenTips and explore what will occur if you choose to click them.

5. Follow these steps to add Open to the Quick Access toolbar:

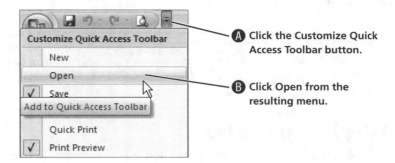

Ⓐ Click the Customize Quick Access Toolbar button.

Ⓑ Click Open from the resulting menu.

6. Notice the new button on the Quick Access toolbar.

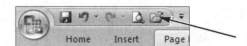

7. Click the Customize Quick Access Toolbar button.

8. Choose Open from the resulting menu.

Entering Data in Excel

You can begin entering data the moment Excel is started. Data is entered into the active cell (the cell with the thick line around it). Text and numbers are used for different purposes in a worksheet. For instance, text entries cannot be used in calculations, whereas number entries can. Text is used for descriptive headings and entries that require alphabetic characters or a combination of alphabetic and numeric characters and spaces. Numbers can be entered directly or can be calculated using formulas. Excel recognizes the data you enter and decides whether the entry is text, a number, or a formula. You will learn about entering formulas in Lesson 3, Working with Formulas and Functions.

Data Types

Entries are defined as one of two main classifications: constant values or formulas. Constant values can be text, numeric, or a combination of both. The one thing that makes an entry constant is that the value does not change when other information changes. Conversely, formula entries display the results of calculations, and a result can change when a value in another cell changes.

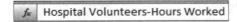

This entry is a constant value; it will not change as other cells are updated.

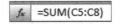

When a formula entry is used, it will refer to one or more cells and will change as the indicated cells are updated.

Completing Cell Entries

Text and numbers are entered by positioning the highlight in the desired cell, typing the desired text or number, and completing the entry. You can use Enter, Tab, or any of the arrow keys ($\rightarrow$, $\leftarrow$, $\uparrow$, $\downarrow$) to complete an entry. The position of the active cell following a cell entry depends on the method by which you complete the entry.

The Enter and Cancel Buttons

The Enter ✓ and Cancel ✗ buttons appear on the Formula Bar whenever you enter or edit an entry. The Enter button completes the entry and keeps the highlight in the current cell. The Cancel button cancels the entry, as does the Esc key.

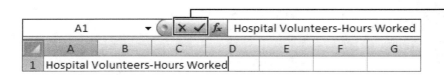

The Cancel and Enter buttons appear when an entry is being entered or edited.

Deleting and Replacing Entries

You can delete an entire entry after it has been completed by clicking in the cell and tapping Delete. Likewise, you can replace an entry by clicking in the cell and typing a new entry. The new entry will replace the original entry. You will learn all about editing entries in Lesson 2, Editing, Viewing, and Printing Worksheets.

Long Text Entries

Text entries often do not fit in a cell. These entries are known as long entries. Excel uses the following rules when deciding how to display long entries:

- If the cell to the right of the long entry is empty, then the long entry displays over the adjacent cell.

- If the cell to the right of the long entry contains an entry, then Excel shortens, or truncates, the display of the long entry.

Keep in mind that Excel does not actually change the long entry; it simply truncates the display of the entry. You can always widen a column to accommodate a long entry.

The entry, Hospital Volunteers-Hours Worked, is a long entry. The entire phrase is entered in cell A1 although it displays over cells A1-D1.

 Hands-On 1.4   Enter Text

1. Make cell A1 active by clicking the mouse pointer ⊕ in it.

2. Type **Hospital Volunteers-Hours Worked** and tap Enter.

3. Click cell A1 and note the appearance of the Formula Bar.

4. Tap the → key to make cell B1 active.

5. Look at the Formula Bar and notice that cell B1 is empty.
   The long entry belongs to cell A1 even though it is displayed over cells A1–D1.

6. Click in cell C3.

7. Type **Wednesday** and tap →| once.

8. Type **Thursday** in cell D3 and tap →|.

9. Enter the remaining text entries shown in the following illustration:

	A	B	C	D	E	F	G
1	Hospital Volunteers-Hours Worked						
2							
3			Wednesd	Thursday	Friday	Saturday	Sunday
4	Gift Shop						
5		Evelyn					
6		Gene					
7		Karel					
8		Bill					
9		Total					
10	Candy Stripers						
11		Ginny					
12		Karel					
13		Ann					
14		Total					
15	Bookmobile						
16		Mohamed					
17		Leticia					
18		Maria					
19		Total					

Working with Numbers

Number entries can contain only the digits 0–9 and a few other characters. Excel initially right-aligns numbers in cells, although you can change this alignment. The following table lists characters that Excel accepts as part of a number entry.

Valid Characters in Number Entries

The digits 0–9

The following characters: + – ( ) , / $ % . *

Number Formats

It isn't necessary to type commas, dollar signs, and other number formats when entering numbers. It's easier to simply enter the numbers and use Excel's formatting commands to add the desired number format(s). You will learn how to format numbers soon.

Decimals and Negative Numbers

You should always type a decimal point if the number you are entering requires one. Likewise, you should precede a negative number entry with a minus (–) sign or enclose it in parentheses ( ).

1. Position the highlight in cell C5.

2. Type **3** but don't complete the entry.

3. Look at the Formula Bar and notice the Cancel ☒ and Enter ☑ buttons.

4. Click the Enter ☑ button to complete the entry.

5. Position the highlight in cell C6 and type **4**, but don't complete the entry.

6. Click the Cancel ☒ button on the Formula Bar to cancel the entry.

7. Type **4** again, but this time tap ⌜Esc⌝ on the keyboard.

8. Type **4** once again, and this time tap ⌑↓⌑ .

9. Enter the remaining numbers shown in the following illustration.

	A	B	C	D	E	F	G
1	Hospital Volunteers-Hours Worked						
2							
3			Wednesd	Thursday	Friday	Saturday	Sunday
4	Gift Shop						
5		Evelyn	3	2	4	0	6
6		Gene	4	2	1	7	3
7		Karel	6	1	2	3	3
8		Bill	3	5	2	2	3
9		Total					
10	Candy Stripers						
11		Ginny	7	0	2	1	4
12		Karel	2	4	1	3	2
13		Ann	4	1	5	2	0
14		Total					
15	Bookmobile						
16		Mohamed	3	6	0	3	2
17		Leticia	1	7	2	2	3
18		Maria	5	2	4	2	0
19		Total					

10. Take a minute to verify that you have correctly entered all the numbers.

Understanding Save Concepts

One important lesson to learn is to save your workbooks early and often! Power outages and careless accidents can result in lost data. The best protection is to save your workbooks every 10 or 15 minutes or after making significant changes. Workbooks are saved to storage locations such as a USB drive, the My Documents folder, a shared network drive, and websites on the Internet.

Storing Your Exercise Files

Throughout this book you will be referred to files in a folder that corresponds to the lesson number you are studying (for example, "the Lesson 02 folder"). You can store your exercise files on various media such as a USB flash drive, the My Documents folder, or a network drive at a school or company. While some figures may display files on a USB flash drive, it is assumed that you will substitute your own location for that shown in the figure.

The Save Command

The Save button on the Quick Access toolbar and →Save initiate the Save command. If a document has been saved previously, Excel replaces the original version with the new, edited version. If a document has never been saved, Excel displays the Save As dialog box. The Save As dialog box lets you specify the name and storage location of the document. You can also use the Save As dialog box to make a copy of a document by saving it under a new name or to a different location. Your filenames can have up to 255 characters, including spaces, giving you the flexibility to create descriptive names for your workbooks.

Save As Options

2007 new!

In Excel 2007, you are given multiple options as to how to save your workbook. How you save it depends on how it will be used and who will be using it. If you are collaborating with someone who has a previous version of Excel installed on his computer, you will need to save the file in the Excel 97-2003 Format. If you wish

If you click the Save As button, the Save As dialog box will be displayed.

If you place your mouse pointer over this menu button, you will see the menu displayed here that gives you additional options for saving your workbook.

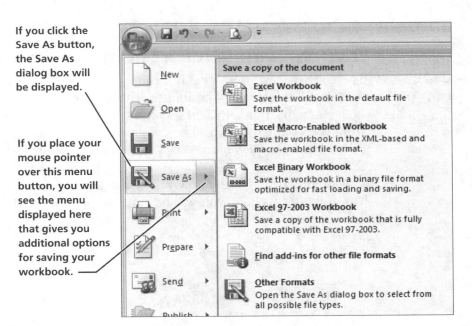

The Save As options available from the Office menu.

to publish your workbook and do not wish for others to make changes to it, you may wish to save it as a PDF file if you have Adobe Acrobat's program. The default format is the Excel 2007 format, which is great to use if everyone who will be utilizing the file has Excel 2007 installed on his computer.

Locating Workbooks

Both the Save As and Open dialog boxes (discussed in Lesson 2, Editing, Viewing, and Printing Worksheets) let you locate workbooks on your local drives, in network locations, and on the web. The Places Bar appears on the left side of the Save As and Open dialog boxes. You can use the Places Bar or the Save In list to locate workbooks, as described in the following illustration.

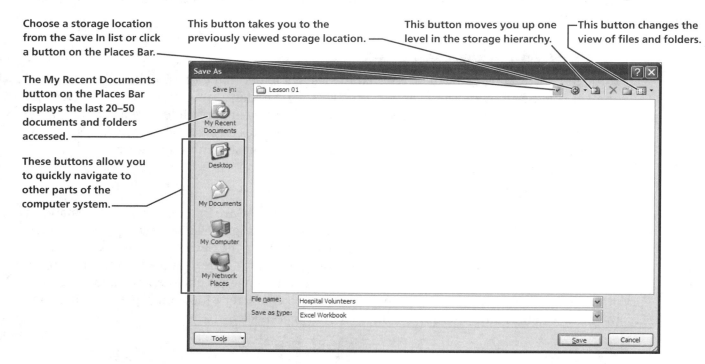

Choose a storage location from the Save In list or click a button on the Places Bar.

This button takes you to the previously viewed storage location.

This button moves you up one level in the storage hierarchy.

This button changes the view of files and folders.

The My Recent Documents button on the Places Bar displays the last 20–50 documents and folders accessed.

These buttons allow you to quickly navigate to other parts of the computer system.

Issuing Commands from the Keyboard

FROM THE KEYBOARD

Ctrl + S to save

There are many times when it is more convenient to issue a command from the keyboard than to chase it down with your mouse. These commands are termed keyboard shortcuts and can help you to be more efficient as you can enter them "on the fly" without removing your fingers from the keyboard. In this book, you will see keyboard shortcuts displayed in a special feature called From the Keyboard. Whenever you issue a keyboard command, you will first hold down the shortcut key (Ctrl, Alt, or Shift) and then tap the additional key to issue the command. This is similar to holding down the Shift key and then tapping a letter to make it capital. Throughout this book you will be asked to use Ctrl + S to save your worksheet.

Hands-On 1.6   Save the Workbook

In this exercise, you will save the workbook created in the previous exercises to your file storage location.

Before You Begin: Navigate to the student web page for this book (labpub.com/learn/excel07_fastcourse1) and download the student exercise files used for this book.

1. Click the Save button on the Quick Access toolbar.

2. Follow these steps to save the workbook:

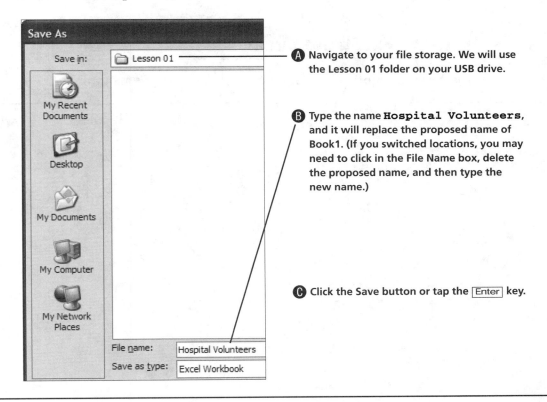

Ⓐ Navigate to your file storage. We will use the Lesson 01 folder on your USB drive.

Ⓑ Type the name **Hospital Volunteers**, and it will replace the proposed name of Book1. (If you switched locations, you may need to click in the File Name box, delete the proposed name, and then type the new name.)

Ⓒ Click the Save button or tap the Enter key.

Closing Workbooks

The 📋→Close command is used to close an open workbook. When you close a workbook that has not been saved, Excel prompts you to save the changes. If you choose Yes at the prompt and the workbook has previously been saved, Excel simply saves the changes. If the workbook is new, Excel displays the Save As dialog box, allowing you to assign a name and storage location to the workbook.

Hands-On 1.7   Close the Workbook

1. Choose 📋→Close.

2. Click the Yes button if Excel asks you if you want to save the changes.

Exiting from Excel

You should close Excel and other programs if you are certain you won't be using them for some time. This will free up memory for other programs. When you close Excel, you will be prompted to save any workbooks that have unsaved edits.

- Click the Office button, and then click ✕ E_xit Excel to exit the program.

- Clicking the Close button ✕ will close only your current Excel 2007 workbook; any other Excel workbooks that are being used will remain open until you close them.

 Hands-On 1.8   **Exit from Excel**

1. Click the Office button, and then click the ✕ E_xit Excel button.

Concepts Review

True/False Questions

1. Each workbook can have a maximum of one worksheet.　　TRUE　FALSE
2. A worksheet is composed of horizontal rows and vertical columns.　　TRUE　FALSE
3. You cannot customize the commands on the Ribbon.　　TRUE　FALSE
4. Text entries can contain spaces.　　TRUE　FALSE
5. Number entries can contain only the digits 0–9. No other characters are permitted.　　TRUE　FALSE
6. A filename can contain spaces.　　TRUE　FALSE
7. Text entries can be used in calculations.　　TRUE　FALSE
8. The Save As command allows you to save your workbook with a different name.　　TRUE　FALSE
9. You should wait to save your workbook until you are done entering all of your data.　　TRUE　FALSE
10. When you click the Close button of the workbook you are working on, it will close all open Excel workbooks.　　TRUE　FALSE

Multiple Choice Questions

1. Which of the following keystrokes moves the highlight to cell A1?
   a. End
   b. Ctrl + Tab
   c. Ctrl + Home
   d. Ctrl + Insert

2. What happens when you insert an entry in the cell to the right of a long text entry?
   a. The display of the long entry is truncated.
   b. The long entry is replaced by the entry in the cell to the right.
   c. It has no effect on the long entry.
   d. None of the above

3. How do you hide the Ribbon?
   a. Choose Home→Hide from the Ribbon
   b. Choose Office button→Hide Ribbon
   c. Double-click the tab that is displayed
   d. Double-click one of the sheet tabs of the workbook

4. What occurs when you tap Esc while entering data into a cell?
   a. The workbook will close.
   b. The entry will be entered and the cell to the right will become active.
   c. Nothing, you can continue entering the data into the cell.
   d. The cell entry will be canceled.

LESSON 2

Editing, Viewing, and Printing Worksheets

In this lesson, you will expand on the basic skills you learned in Lesson 1. You will learn various methods of editing worksheets: replacing and deleting entries, using Undo and Redo, working with AutoCorrect, and more. You will also learn about printing Excel worksheets and working with different views. When you have finished this lesson, you will have developed the skills necessary to produce carefully edited and proofed worksheets.

LESSON OBJECTIVES

After studying this lesson, you will be able to:

- Open and edit a workbook file
- Use a variety of techniques to select cells and ranges
- Move and copy cell entries
- Undo and redo commands
- Clear cell contents, including formatting
- Use AutoFill and AutoComplete
- Work with various Excel views and the zoom feature
- Preview your worksheet before printing
- Print your worksheet, including printing specific sections of your worksheet

LESSON TIMING

- Concepts/Hands-On: 1 hr 15 min
- Concepts Review: 15 min
- Total: 1 hr 30 min

CASE STUDY: CREATING A BASIC LIST IN EXCEL

Ken Hazell is the owner of Carmel Automotive Repair. He realizes that Excel would be the best tool to keep track of his employees' personal data. Excel can be used as a simple database to keep track of lists of employees, inventory, or other items. Microsoft Excel is an important tool for any entrepreneur in today's highly competitive business world.

Opening Workbooks

The Office button →Open command displays the Open dialog box. The Open dialog box lets you navigate to any storage location and open previously saved workbooks. Once a workbook is open, you can browse it, print it, and make editing changes. The organization and layout of the Open dialog box are similar to those of the Save As dialog box.

FROM THE KEYBOARD
Ctrl+O to open

Hands-On 2.1   Open the Workbook

1. Start Excel.

2. Click the Office button, and then choose the Open command.

3. Follow these steps to open the CAR Employee Roster workbook:

Ⓐ Navigate to your file storage location. This will likely be your USB flash drive.

Ⓑ Double-click to open the Lesson 02 folder.

Name ▲
📁 Lesson 02
📁 Lesson 03
📁 Lesson 04

Open

Look in: 📁 Lesson 02

Ⓒ Click to choose the CAR Employee Roster file.

My Recent Documents

Name ▲
as-Bonuses
as-Menu
CAR Employee Roster

Ⓓ Click the Open button.

Editing Entries

You can edit the active cell by clicking in the Formula Bar and making the desired changes. You can also double-click a cell and edit the contents directly there. This technique is known as in-cell editing.

Replacing Entries

Editing an entry is efficient if the entry is so long that retyping it would be time-consuming. Editing can also be helpful when working with complex formulas and other functions that are difficult to re-create. If the entry requires little typing, however, it is usually easier to simply retype it. If you retype an entry, the new entry will be replace whatever is contained in the cell.

Deleting Characters

Use the Delete and Backspace keys to edit entries in the Formula Bar and within a cell. The Delete key removes the character to the right of the insertion point, while the Backspace key removes the character to the left of the insertion point.

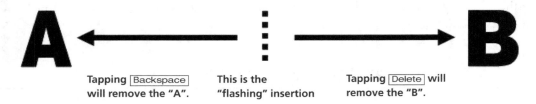

A ← : → **B**

Tapping Backspace will remove the "A".

This is the "flashing" insertion

Tapping Delete will remove the "B".

 ## Hands-On 2.2   Edit Entries

1. Click cell A2 to select it.

2. Follow these steps to edit cell A2 using the Formula Bar:

   A Click in the Formula Bar just to the right of the word *List*.

   ⊙ ✗ ✓ *fx*   Employee Roster

   B Tap Backspace four times to remove the word *List*, and then type **Roster**.

   C Click the Enter button.

3. Click cell D4.

4. Type **Employment Date** and tap Enter.

5. Double-click cell A7 (the cell with the name Isabella Soprano).

6. Use the mouse or the → key to position the flashing insertion point to the right of the last name, Soprano.

7. Type **–Birdsell**, and then tap Enter to complete the change.

8. Click the Save 🖫 button to update the changes.

Selecting Cells and Ranges

When you want to change something in a worksheet—for instance, move, copy, delete, format, or print specific data—you must first select the cell(s). The most efficient way to select cells is with the mouse, though you can also use the keyboard method. You can select one or many cells. A group of contiguous (adjacent) cells is called a range.

Excel Ranges

In the last lesson, you learned that each cell has a reference. For example, A1 refers to the first cell in a worksheet. Likewise, a range reference specifies the cells included within a range. The range reference includes the first and last cells in the range separated by a colon (:). For example, the range A4:E4 includes all cells between A4 and E4 inclusive. The following illustration highlights several ranges and their corresponding range references.

	A6	▼		f_x	Christina Chu		
	A		**B**	**C**	**D**	**E**	
1	Carmel Automotive Repair						
2	Employee Roster						
3							
4	Name		Phone	Position	Employment Dat	Lock-up Day	
5	Ken Hazell		619-555-3224	Owner			
6	Christina Chu		858-555-3098	Front Office	5/25/2004		
7	Isabella Soprano-Birdsell		619-555-3309	Front Office	3/28/2003		
8	Derek Navarro		951-555-0826	Front Office	8/3/2005		
9	Jason Rogers		858-555-4987	Front Office	1/5/1999		
10	Matt Bernardo		858-555-0211	Front Office	4/13/2001		
11	Meredith Baxter		858-555-1002	Mechanic	5/10/2003		
12	George Springhurst		858-555-0021	Mechanic	10/30/2002		
13	Preston Washington		760-555-3876	Mechanic	12/24/2003		
14	Steve Porter		619-555-4016	Mechanic	4/23/2002		
15	David Scott		760-555-0728	Mechanic	7/29/2000		

Range A1:A2 — (rows 1–2)
Range A4:E4 — (row 4)
Range A6:D10 — (rows 6–10)

The selected ranges in the worksheet are shaded, as displayed above. In addition, the first cell in the last range selected, A6, shows no shading and has an outline around it. This indicates that it is the active cell, which is displayed in the Name box and Formula Bar.

Hands-On 2.3   Practice Making Selections

1. Position the mouse pointer ✛ over cell A4.

2. Press and hold down the left mouse button while dragging the mouse to the right until the range A4:E4 is selected, and then release the mouse button.

3. Click once anywhere in the worksheet to deselect the cells.

4. Follow these steps to select two ranges:

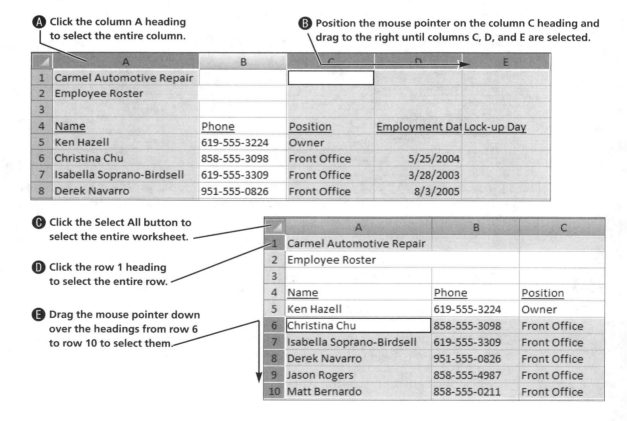

Ⓐ Select the range A4:E4 as you did in steps 1 and 2 above.

Ⓑ Press and hold down the Ctrl key while dragging to select the range A6:D10.

	A	B	C	D	E
1	Carmel Automotive Repair				
2	Employee Roster				
3					
4	Name	Phone	Position	Employment Dat	Lock-up Day
5	Ken Hazell	619-555-3224	Owner		
6	Christina Chu	858-555-3098	Front Office	5/25/2004	
7	Isabella Soprano-Birdsell	619-555-3309	Front Office	3/28/2003	
8	Derek Navarro	951-555-0826	Front Office	8/3/2005	
9	Jason Rogers	858-555-4987	Front Office	1/5/1999	
10	Matt Bernardo	858-555-0211	Front Office	4/13/2001	

Ⓒ Release the Ctrl key after the second range is selected.

5. Press and hold down the Ctrl key while you select another range, and then release the Ctrl key.

6. Make sure you have released the Ctrl key, and then click once anywhere on the worksheet to deselect the ranges.

7. Follow these steps to select various rows and columns:

Ⓐ Click the column A heading to select the entire column.

Ⓑ Position the mouse pointer on the column C heading and drag to the right until columns C, D, and E are selected.

	A	B	C	D	E
1	Carmel Automotive Repair				
2	Employee Roster				
3					
4	Name	Phone	Position	Employment Dat	Lock-up Day
5	Ken Hazell	619-555-3224	Owner		
6	Christina Chu	858-555-3098	Front Office	5/25/2004	
7	Isabella Soprano-Birdsell	619-555-3309	Front Office	3/28/2003	
8	Derek Navarro	951-555-0826	Front Office	8/3/2005	

Ⓒ Click the Select All button to select the entire worksheet.

Ⓓ Click the row 1 heading to select the entire row.

Ⓔ Drag the mouse pointer down over the headings from row 6 to row 10 to select them.

	A	B	C
1	Carmel Automotive Repair		
2	Employee Roster		
3			
4	Name	Phone	Position
5	Ken Hazell	619-555-3224	Owner
6	Christina Chu	858-555-3098	Front Office
7	Isabella Soprano-Birdsell	619-555-3309	Front Office
8	Derek Navarro	951-555-0826	Front Office
9	Jason Rogers	858-555-4987	Front Office
10	Matt Bernardo	858-555-0211	Front Office

8. Follow these steps to use keyboard techniques to select cells:

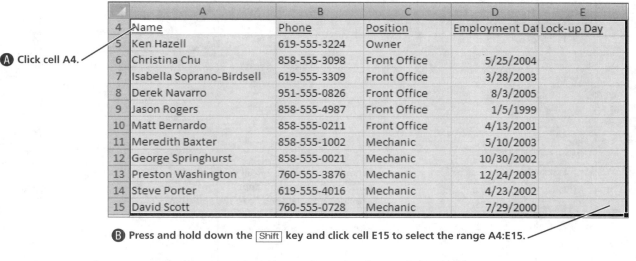

A Click cell A4.

	A	B	C	D	E
4	Name	Phone	Position	Employment Dat	Lock-up Day
5	Ken Hazell	619-555-3224	Owner		
6	Christina Chu	858-555-3098	Front Office	5/25/2004	
7	Isabella Soprano-Birdsell	619-555-3309	Front Office	3/28/2003	
8	Derek Navarro	951-555-0826	Front Office	8/3/2005	
9	Jason Rogers	858-555-4987	Front Office	1/5/1999	
10	Matt Bernardo	858-555-0211	Front Office	4/13/2001	
11	Meredith Baxter	858-555-1002	Mechanic	5/10/2003	
12	George Springhurst	858-555-0021	Mechanic	10/30/2002	
13	Preston Washington	760-555-3876	Mechanic	12/24/2003	
14	Steve Porter	619-555-4016	Mechanic	4/23/2002	
15	David Scott	760-555-0728	Mechanic	7/29/2000	

B Press and hold down the Shift **key and click cell E15 to select the range A4:E15.**

C Click cell A11.

	A	B	C	D
11	Meredith Baxter	858-555-1002	Mechanic	5/10/2003
12	George Springhurst	858-555-0021	Mechanic	10/30/2002
13	Preston Washington	760-555-3876	Mechanic	12/24/2003
14	Steve Porter	619-555-4016	Mechanic	4/23/2002
15	David Scott	760-555-0728	Mechanic	7/29/2000

D Press and hold down the Shift **key, and then tap** → **three times and** ↓ **four times.**

9. Take a few moments to practice selection techniques. See if you can select any portion of a worksheet you wish.

Working with Cut, Copy, and Paste

The Cut, Copy, and Paste commands are available in all Office 2007 applications. With Cut, Copy, and Paste, you can move or copy cells within a worksheet, between worksheets, or between different Office applications. For example, you could use the Copy command to copy a range from one worksheet and the Paste command to paste the range into another worksheet. Cut, Copy, and Paste are most efficient for moving or copying cells a long distance within a worksheet or between worksheets. Cut, Copy, and Paste are easy to use if you remember the following guidelines:

FROM THE KEYBOARD

Ctrl + C to copy
Ctrl + X to cut
Ctrl + V to paste

- You must select cells before issuing a Cut or Copy command.

- You must position the highlight at the desired location before issuing the Paste command. This is important because the range you paste will overwrite any cells in the paste area.

You can also right-click on a cell or range of cells in order to get a shortcut menu specific to the selection. The Cut, Copy, and Paste commands are available on this menu as well. There are many ways to issue commands; your job is to simply figure out which method works best for you!

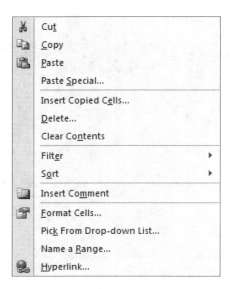

When you right-click a cell or range of cells, a shortcut menu appears that provides options specific to the selection. Notice that you can choose to Cut, Copy, and Paste from this menu.

The Office Clipboard

The Office Clipboard lets you collect items from any Office worksheet or program and paste them into any other Office document. For example, you can collect a paragraph from a Word document, data from an Excel worksheet, and a graphic from a PowerPoint slide and then paste them all into a new Word document. The Office Clipboard can also be used within a single application like Excel to collect several items and then paste them as desired. The Office Clipboard can hold up to 24 items.

How It Works

You can place items on the Office Clipboard using the standard Cut and Copy commands; however, the Office Clipboard task pane must first be displayed. It is displayed by clicking the Launcher button in the Clipboard area of the Home Ribbon.

Moving Cells via Drag and Drop

Drag and Drop produces the same results as Cut, Copy, and Paste. However, Drag and Drop is usually more efficient if you are moving or copying entries a short distance within the same worksheet. If the original location and new destination are both visible in the current window, then it is usually easier to use Drag and Drop. With Drag and Drop, you select the cells you wish to move or copy, and then you point to the edge of the selected range and drag the range to the desired destination. If you press the Ctrl key while dragging the selected area, the cells are copied to the destination. Drag and Drop does not place items on the Office Clipboard, however, so you will want to use either the Cut or the Copy command if you wish to work with the Clipboard.

Editing Cells via Right-Dragging

Right-dragging is a variation of the Drag and Drop technique. Many beginners find Drag and Drop difficult to use because they have difficulty controlling the mouse. This difficulty is compounded if they are trying to copy entries using Drag and Drop. This is because copying requires the [Ctrl] key to be held while the selected range is dragged. With the right-drag method, the right mouse button is used when dragging. When the right mouse button is released at the destination, a pop-up menu appears. The pop-up menu gives you several options including Move, Copy, and Cancel. This provides more control because there is no need to use the [Ctrl] key when copying, and you have the option of canceling the move or copy.

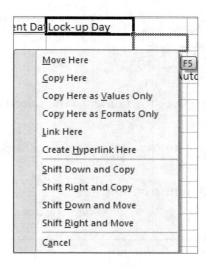

When you right-drag and drop, you will receive a pop-up menu at the destination so that you can choose whether to move or copy the data. Many of the rest of the options displayed will be covered in subsequent lessons.

 ## Hands-On 2.4   Move and Copy Selections

1. Click cell A1 to select it.

2. Make sure the Home tab is displayed, locate the Clipboard command group, and then click the Copy ⊞ button on the Ribbon.

3. Click cell C2.

4. Choose Home→Clipboard→Paste ⊟ from the Ribbon to paste the selection in cell C2.

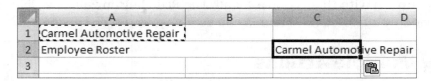

5. Right-click cell C2.

6. Choose Cut from the shortcut menu.

7. Right-click cell E2 and choose Paste from the shortcut menu.

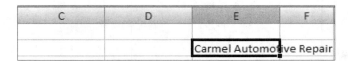

8. Follow these steps to move the contents of cell E2 via drag and drop:

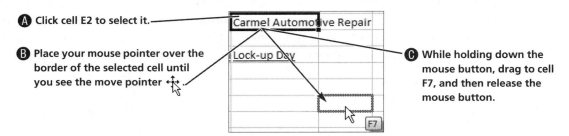

Ⓐ Click cell E2 to select it.

Ⓑ Place your mouse pointer over the border of the selected cell until you see the move pointer

Ⓒ While holding down the mouse button, drag to cell F7, and then release the mouse button.

9. Select cell E4, and then place your mouse pointer over the border of the selected cell until you see the move pointer as shown at right.

10. Start dragging with the right (not the left) mouse button. Keep the right mouse button held down until told to release it in the next step.

11. Drag down to cell F5, and then release the right mouse button.

12. Choose Copy Here from the pop-up menu.

Using Undo and Redo

Excel's Undo button lets you reverse actions that have occurred in Excel. You can reverse simple actions such as accidentally deleting a cell's content or more complex actions such as deleting an entire row. Most actions can be undone, but those that cannot include printing and saving workbooks. The Undo command can become your best friend when you have to undo an action that you are not sure how you issued. Don't you wish life had an undo button at times!

The Redo button reverses an Undo command. Use Redo when you undo an action but then decide to go through with that action after all. The Redo button will be visible on the Quick Access toolbar only after you have undone an action.

Undoing Multiple Actions

FROM THE KEYBOARD
Ctrl+Z to undo
Ctrl+Y to redo
Clicking the arrow on the Undo button displays a list of actions that can be undone. You can undo multiple actions by dragging the mouse over the desired actions. However, you must undo actions in the order in which they appear on the drop-down list.

When you click the arrow on the Undo button, you will see a list of previous commands.

Limitations to "Undoing"

In Excel, there are some times when the Undo command will not work. If you click the Office button and choose any command, it cannot be undone (such as saving a workbook). When an action cannot be undone, Excel will change the Undo ScreenTip to "Can't Undo."

Hands-On 2.5   Reverse Actions

1. Click the column A heading to select the entire column.

2. Tap Delete.

3. Click Undo ⟲ to restore the entry.

4. Follow these steps to undo the last four commands from the previous section:

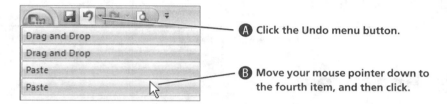

A Click the Undo menu button.

B Move your mouse pointer down to the fourth item, and then click.

5. Click the Redo ⟳ button four times to restore the four actions that you "undid."

6. Use Ctrl+S to save the changes, but don't close the workbook.

Clearing Cell Contents and Formats

In Excel, you can format cell content by changing the font style, size, and color. You can also add enhancements such as bold, italics, and underline. Cells with numeric data can be formatted as currency, dates, times, percents, and more. In Lesson 4, Formatting the Contents of Cells you will learn how to format cells.

FROM THE KEYBOARD
Delete to clear cell contents

Clicking the Clear ✐▾ button displays a menu that lets you clear content, formats, and comments from cells. The submenu also contains an All option that clears all of these items from the selected cell(s).

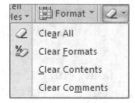

Clicking the Clear button in the Editing section of the Home Ribbon will display a menu that shows all of the options for clearing cell contents.

One of the most useful functions of Excel's Clear command is removing numeric value formats. This is because once a cell is formatted as a particular numeric format, such as a date or currency, Excel remembers that formatting even if the cell contents are deleted.

Hands-On 2.6   Clear Cell Contents and Formatting

1. Click cell F5.

2. Choose Home→Editing→Clear 🖉⁻ from the Ribbon, choose Clear Formats, and then tap Enter twice.

3. Click the Undo 🔄 button on the Quick Access toolbar.

4. Ensure that cell F5 is selected, and then click the Clear 🖉⁻ button and choose Clear All.

5. Type your name and tap Enter.

6. Use Ctrl + Z to undo the typing of your name.

7. Click cell F7 and tap Delete.

8. Click the Save 💾 button.

Using Auto Features

Excel offers many "auto" features that help you to work more efficiently. AutoFill allows you to quickly fill a range of cells. AutoComplete makes it easy to enter long entries by typing an acronym or series of characters, which are "converted" to the desired entry. AutoCorrect can also assist in correcting commonly misspelled words.

Working with AutoFill

AutoFill allows you to quickly extend a series, copy data, or copy a formula into adjacent cells by selecting cells and dragging the fill handle. You will learn about using AutoFill to copy formulas in Lesson 3, Working with Formulas and Functions If the selected cell does not contain data that AutoFill recognizes as a series, the data will simply be copied into the adjacent cells. The fill handle is a small black square at the bottom-right corner of the active cell. A black cross appears when you position the mouse pointer on the fill handle. You can drag the fill handle to fill adjacent cells as described below.

■ Copy an entry—If the entry in the active cell is a number, a formula, or a text entry, the fill handle copies the entry to adjacent cells.

■ Expand a repeating series of numbers—If you select two or more cells containing numbers, Excel assumes you want to expand a repeating series. For example, if you select two cells containing the numbers 5 and 10 and drag the fill handle, Excel will fill the adjacent cells with the numbers 15, 20, 25, etc.

■ AutoFill of date entries—If the active cell contains any type of date entry, Excel will determine the increment of the date value and fill in the adjacent cells. For example, if the current cell contains the entry Q1 and you drag the fill handle, AutoFill will insert the entries Q2, Q3, and Q4 in the adjacent cells.

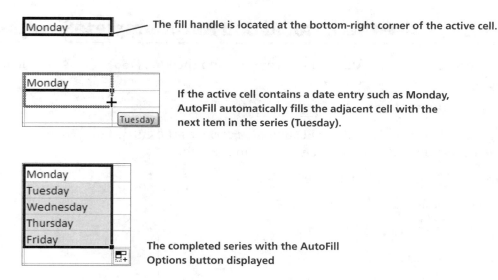

The fill handle is located at the bottom-right corner of the active cell.

If the active cell contains a date entry such as Monday, AutoFill automatically fills the adjacent cell with the next item in the series (Tuesday).

The completed series with the AutoFill Options button displayed

AutoFill Options

The AutoFill Options ⊞ button appears below your filled selection after you fill cells in a worksheet. A menu of fill options appears when you click the button.

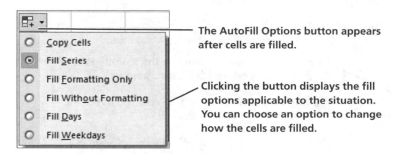

The AutoFill Options button appears after cells are filled.

Clicking the button displays the fill options applicable to the situation. You can choose an option to change how the cells are filled.

If you choose to Fill without Formatting, you can fill cells without copying the formatting from the original cell.

AutoComplete vs. AutoFill

The AutoComplete feature is useful when you want the same entry repeated more than once in a column. AutoFill allows you to select a cell and fill in entries either by completing a series or copying the source cell, whereas AutoComplete works within a cell as you type. If the first few characters you type match another entry in the column, then AutoComplete will offer to complete the entry for you. You accept the offer by tapping Enter or reject the offer by typing the remainder of the entry yourself.

| 15 | David Scott | 760-555-0728 | Mechanic |
| 16 | Charlie Simpson | 858-555-3718 | mechanic |

In this situation, an "m" was typed and the AutoComplete feature kicked into gear, suggesting that you may be interested in completing the entry as *Mechanic* since you have already typed that entry earlier in the column. In order to accept *Mechanic* as the entry, you would simply tap Enter.

1. Click cell A16 and type **Charlie Simpson**, and then tap ⌗Tab⌗ to move to the next cell to the right.

2. Type **858-555-3718** and tap ⌗Tab⌗.

3. Type **m** and notice that Excel will suggest *Mechanic* as the entry. Tap ⌗Tab⌗ to accept the suggestion and move to the next cell to the right.

4. Type today's date, and then type ⌗Enter⌗.

5. Type **Leisa Malimali** and tap ⌗Tab⌗.

6. Type **619-555-4017** and tap ⌗Tab⌗.

7. Type **M** in cell C17.

8. Continue typing **anager** and tap ⌗Tab⌗.

9. Type today's date and tap ⌗Enter⌗.

10. Click cell E6.

11. Type **Monday**, and then click the Enter ✓ button.

12. Follow these steps to fill the adjacent cells:

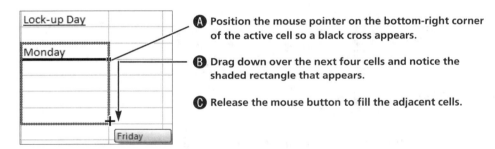

Ⓐ Position the mouse pointer on the bottom-right corner of the active cell so a black cross appears.

Ⓑ Drag down over the next four cells and notice the shaded rectangle that appears.

Ⓒ Release the mouse button to fill the adjacent cells.

13. Click the AutoFill Options button and note the various fill options.

14. For now, just tap ⌗Esc⌗ to dismiss the menu.

Exploring the Many Views of Excel

When you change the view in Excel, it does not change how the worksheet will print. For instance, if you change the zoom to 300%, the worksheet will appear much larger on the screen but will still print normally. There are other views in Excel that will aid you in working with your file and assist you in making changes to the final printed worksheet. There is an additional view option that will be covered in *FastCourse Excel 2007: Level 2*, Page Break Preview, that allows you to set where pages will break when printed.

The View tab on the Ribbon provides options for how to view your workbook, which screen elements to show or hide, control of the zoom, and other window display options such as Freeze Panes and Split Window. This lesson will cover Page Layout view and Zoom. Remember that your Ribbon may appear differently, depending on the size of your Excel window.

Working in Page Layout View

Page Layout view allows you to see how your spreadsheet will appear when you print it, page by page. You can even add headers and footers and edit your worksheet in this view.

Zooming the View

The Zoom control lets you zoom in to get a close-up view of a worksheet and zoom out to see the full view. Zooming changes the size of the onscreen worksheet but has no effect on the printed worksheet. You can zoom from 10% to 400%.

You can move the slider to change the zoom.

You can also click the Zoom Out ⊖ and Zoom In ⊕ buttons to change the zoom.

Clicking the Zoom button will open the Zoom dialog box so that you can set the zoom more precisely.

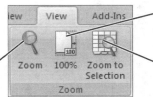

The 100% button allows you to quickly return the zoom to 100%.

The Zoom to Selection button on the Ribbon will customize the zoom to display the selected range of cells.

1. Follow these steps to adjust the zoom percentage:

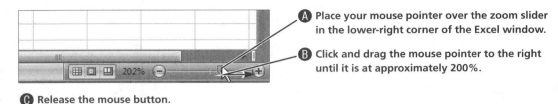

A Place your mouse pointer over the zoom slider in the lower-right corner of the Excel window.

B Click and drag the mouse pointer to the right until it is at approximately 200%.

C Release the mouse button.

2. Click the Zoom Out ⊖ button several times until the zoom displays 100%.

3. Drag to select the range A1:E17.

4. Click the View tab to display the View Ribbon.

5. Click the Zoom to Selection button in the Zoom area of the Ribbon.

6. Choose View→Zoom→100% from the Ribbon.

7. Choose View→Workbook Views→Page Layout View from the Ribbon.

8. Choose View→Workbook Views→Normal from the Ribbon.

Printing Worksheets

Excel gives you many ways to print your work. The method you choose depends on what you want to print. The basic print command, for instance, offers you print options such as printing specified pages, a selected range, or the entire workbook. Additional choices include printing multiple copies and collating options.

The Quick Print 🖶 button can be added to the Quick Access toolbar. When clicked, it will print one copy of the entire worksheet. For large workbooks in which you frequently want to print only a certain selection, you can print a selection or set a print area. Before printing, you can use Print Preview or Page Layout view to see what is going to be printed. In *FastCourse Excel 2007: Level 2*, you will learn how to change page setup options such as changing the print orientation, printing column headings on every page, setting the print area, and many others.

Print Preview

The Print Preview command displays the Print Preview window. Print Preview lets you see exactly how a worksheet will look when printed. Print Preview can save time, paper, and wear and tear on your printer. It is especially useful when printing large worksheets and those with charts and intricate formatting. It is always wise to preview a large or complex worksheet before sending it to the printer. When you display the Print Preview window, the normal Ribbons are replaced by a Print Preview Ribbon. Print Preview is a very valuable tool in looking at how your worksheet will look when printed, but you are not able to edit your worksheet when you are in print preview mode (you will want to use Page Layout view for this purpose).

Choose Print to access the Print dialog box.

Choose Page Setup to access the Page Setup dialog box.

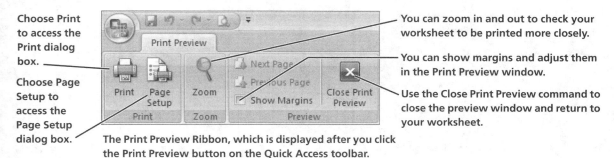

You can zoom in and out to check your worksheet to be printed more closely.

You can show margins and adjust them in the Print Preview window.

Use the Close Print Preview command to close the preview window and return to your worksheet.

The Print Preview Ribbon, which is displayed after you click the Print Preview button on the Quick Access toolbar.

Print the Worksheet

 You can customize your Quick Access toolbar to include the Quick Print button, which sends the entire worksheet to the current printer. You must display the Print dialog box if you want to change printers, adjust the number of copies to be printed, or set other printing options such as printing only selected cells. The Print dialog box is displayed by clicking the Office button and choosing the Print command. The following illustration explains the most important options available in the Print dialog box.

You select the printer to which you wish to print here.

Choose whether to print the entire worksheet or specific pages.

Decide exactly what you wish to print.

You can access the Print Preview window from the Print dialog box.

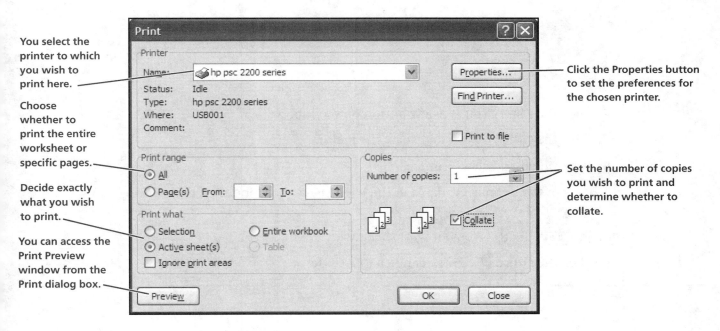

Click the Properties button to set the preferences for the chosen printer.

Set the number of copies you wish to print and determine whether to collate.

Printing Selections

Many times you will want to print only a range of cells. You can do this by selecting the desired cells, displaying the Print dialog box, choosing to print the selection, and clicking OK. You also use this technique to print nonadjacent selections within a worksheet or workbook. For example, use this technique to print two non-adjacent sections of a worksheet or two or more sections on different worksheets. Non-adjacent selections print on separate pages.

FROM THE KEYBOARD
Ctrl + P to print

Hands-On 2.9   Preview and Print a Worksheet

1. Follow these steps to preview the worksheet before printing:

Ⓐ Click the Office button.

Ⓑ Trace your mouse down to the arrow to the right of Print.

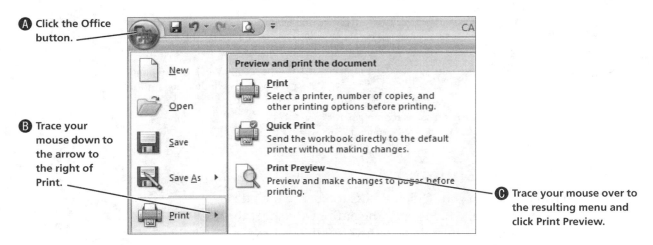

Ⓒ Trace your mouse over to the resulting menu and click Print Preview.

2. Click the Zoom button to zoom in on your worksheet and then again to zoom out.

3. Click in the box to the left of Show Margins.

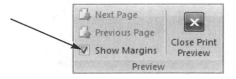

4. Click the Close Print Preview button on the Ribbon.

5. Click the Office button to display the menu.

6. Trace down and click Print.

7. Look at the options available in the Print Dialog box, and then click OK to print the worksheet.

8. Tap Ctrl + s to save your worksheet.

9. Click the Office 🔘 button and choose Close.

Concepts Review

True/False Questions

1. Excel allows you to undo all commands issued.   TRUE   FALSE

2. Double-clicking in a cell lets you revise the contents of the cell without replacing the entire contents.   TRUE   FALSE

3. When you delete the contents of a cell using the Delete key on the keyboard, the formatting remains.   TRUE   FALSE

4. If you drag and drop using the left mouse button, you will be able to choose the command to issue when the mouse button is released.   TRUE   FALSE

5. You cannot delete the formats in a cell without deleting the contents as well.   TRUE   FALSE

6. You select an entire row by clicking the row header.   TRUE   FALSE

7. Page Layout view allows you to add headings and footers to your worksheet.   TRUE   FALSE

8. You can print a group of cells without printing the entire worksheet.   TRUE   FALSE

9. Changing the zoom in a worksheet will change the way it prints.   TRUE   FALSE

10. AutoFill allows you to easily enter contents into cells that have been entered into another cell in the column.   TRUE   FALSE

Multiple Choice Questions

1. What happens when you enter text in a cell that already contains an entry?
   a. The text replaces the original entry.
   b. Excel rejects the new entry, keeping the original entry intact.
   c. The cell contains both the original entry and the new entry.
   d. None of the above

2. Which command can be issued when you click the Clear button on the Ribbon?
   a. Clear the entire worksheet.
   b. Clear the formatting from a cell.
   c. Clear the formula from a cell.
   d. None of the above

3. What must you do before issuing a Cut or Copy command?
   a. Choose Home→Clipboard→Cut, or Home→ Clipboard→ Copy from the Ribbon.
   b. Double-click the cell from which you wish to cut or copy.
   c. Click the column header of the cell from which you wish to cut or copy.
   d. Select the cell(s) you wish to cut or copy.

4. What does the Print Preview view allow you to do?
   a. Add headers and footers to your worksheet.
   b. Observe how your spreadsheet will look when printed.
   c. Edit your worksheet.
   d. Both a and b

LESSON 3

Working with Formulas and Functions

The magic of the Excel spreadsheet lies in its ability to crunch numbers and make sense of data. The heart of this magic lies in the formulas and functions that are used for this number crunching. In this lesson, you will be introduced to creating and modifying basic formulas and functions in Excel. You will learn how to reference cells in formulas as well as how to use another automated feature of Excel, AutoSum. Sit back and relax as you begin to discover the true power of Excel.

LESSON OBJECTIVES

After studying this lesson, you will be able to:

- Create formulas to calculate values, utilizing the proper syntax and order of operations
- Use a variety of methods to create statistical functions to determine the sum, average, maximum, and minimum of a range of numbers
- Use relative and absolute cell references in formulas and functions
- Modify and copy formulas and functions
- Display the formulas contained within cells rather than the resulting value

LESSON TIMING

- Concepts/Hands-On: 1 hr 15 min
- Concepts Review: 15 min
- Total: 1 hr 30 min

CASE STUDY: CREATING A SPREADSHEET WITH FORMULAS

The Big Bear Mountain Inn is a 200-room hotel located next to a ski resort. The manager of the hotel, Glen Livingston, has asked the accountant, Tammy McJagger, to prepare commission and monthly projected profit reports for the first quarter. Commissions are not paid for in-house bookings but are paid to outside agencies who book rooms for the inn.

Tammy has set up a workbook with two worksheets, one to track commissions and the other to help Glen view how the projected profit changes based on occupancy. Your job will be to help Tammy create the necessary formulas and functions for the workbook.

Working with Formulas and Functions

A formula is simply a math problem done in Excel. You can add, subtract, multiply, divide, and group numbers and cell contents in order to make your data work for you. A function is a prewritten formula that helps to simplify complex procedures, both for numbers and for text. For instance, a function can be used to sum a group of numbers, to determine the payment amount on a loan, and to search for text.

Using AutoSum

The power of Excel becomes apparent when you begin using formulas and functions. The most common type of calculation is summing a column or row of numbers. In fact, this type of calculation is so common that Excel provides the AutoSum feature specifically for this purpose.

FROM THE KEYBOARD

Alt + = for Autosum

The **Σ AutoSum ▾** button on the Home tab automatically sums a column or row of numbers. When you click AutoSum, Excel proposes a range of cells. Excel will first look "up" for a range to sum, and if a range is not found there, it will next look left. You can accept the proposed range or drag in the worksheet to select a different range. When you complete the entry, Excel places a SUM function in the worksheet, which adds the numbers in the range.

You can include empty cells in the range that you wish to AutoSum, although if you are averaging a range of cells you will want to include only those cells with a value that should be included in the average.

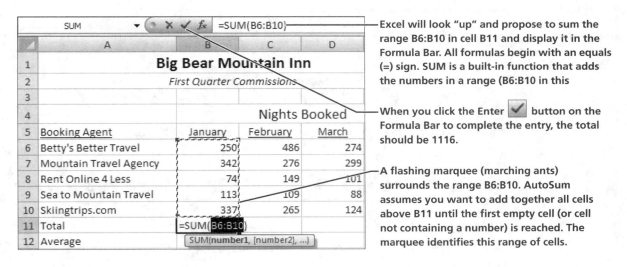

Excel will look "up" and propose to sum the range B6:B10 in cell B11 and display it in the Formula Bar. All formulas begin with an equals (=) sign. SUM is a built-in function that adds the numbers in a range (B6:B10 in this

When you click the Enter ✔ button on the Formula Bar to complete the entry, the total should be 1116.

A flashing marquee (marching ants) surrounds the range B6:B10. AutoSum assumes you want to add together all cells above B11 until the first empty cell (or cell not containing a number) is reached. The marquee identifies this range of cells.

Other Functions Available Through the AutoSum Button

The AutoSum button does not stop at simply summing a group of numbers. The following statistical functions are also available as automated features: average, count numbers, maximum, and minimum.

Status Bar Functions and Customization

The status bar, which is displayed at the bottom of the Excel window, allows you to view information about a range of numbers without actually inserting a function in the worksheet. You can customize the status bar to display the following functions: Average, Count, Numerical Count, Minimum, Maximum, and Sum. To customize the status bar, right-click anywhere on it and click to add or remove features. Other than functions, you can also customize additional features of the status bar such as zoom, signatures, overtype mode, and macros.

The range of B6:D10 has been selected in the worksheet.

When you right-click on the status bar, you will get a menu by which you can customize the status bar.

Notice that the sum in cell E11 matches the sum displayed on the status bar.

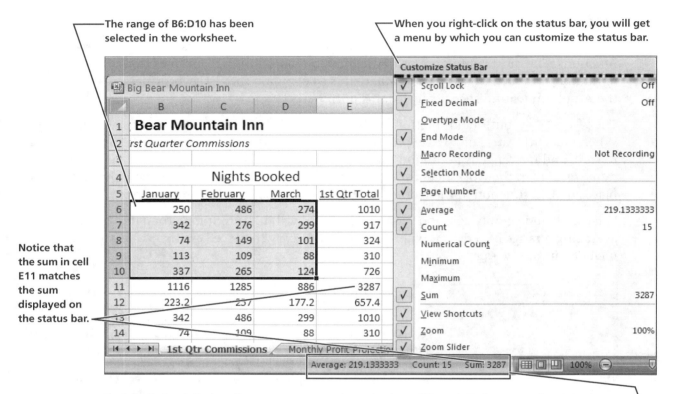

By default, Excel displays the sum, average, and count values of the selected range on the status bar.

Hands-On 3.1   Use AutoSum and Status Bar Functions

1. Start Excel.

2. Open the Big Bear Mountain Inn workbook from the Lesson 03 folder in your file storage location.

3. Click cell B11.

4. Choose Home→Editing→Sum Σ from the Ribbon.

5. Follow these steps to complete the AutoSum formula.

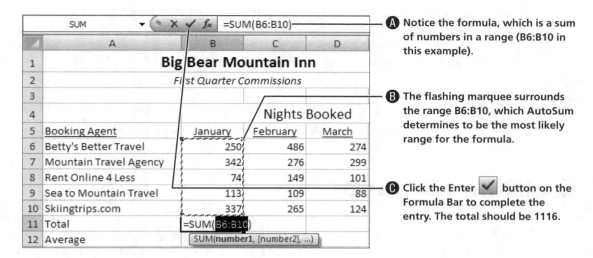

Ⓐ Notice the formula, which is a sum of numbers in a range (B6:B10 in this example).

Ⓑ The flashing marquee surrounds the range B6:B10, which AutoSum determines to be the most likely range for the formula.

Ⓒ Click the Enter ✔ button on the Formula Bar to complete the entry. The total should be 1116.

6. Click in cell C11.

7. Choose Home→Editing→Sum **Σ** from the Ribbon and complete ✔ the entry.

8. Use the preceding technique to calculate the column total in cell D11.

9. Click in cell E6.

10. Choose Home→Editing→Sum **Σ** from the Ribbon.

11. Tap ⌈Enter⌋ to complete the entry.

12. Use the preceding technique to calculate the row total in cell E7.

13. Click in cell E8, and then choose Home→Editing→Sum **Σ** from the Ribbon.

14. Follow these steps to override the proposed range:

Ⓐ Position the mouse pointer over cell B8, and then click and drag to the right until the range B8:D8 is selected.

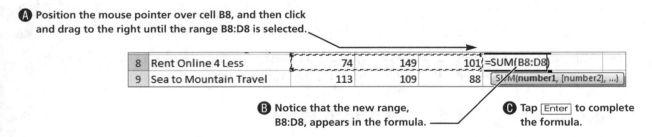

Ⓑ Notice that the new range, B8:D8, appears in the formula.

Ⓒ Tap ⌈Enter⌋ to complete the formula.

15. Follow these steps to AutoFill the formula in cell E8 to the three cells below it:

Ⓐ Click cell E8.

Ⓑ Position your mouse pointer over the fill handle at the bottom-right corner of the cell until you see the thin cross, and then press the left mouse button and drag down through cell E11.

Ⓒ Release the mouse button to fill the formula into the cells.

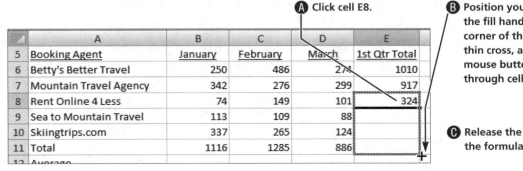

16. Drag to select the range B6:D10.

17. Look at the Status bar to see the sum value displayed by AutoCalculate.

18. Click the save button, but leave the spreadsheet open for the next exercise.

Creating Formulas

You have already learned how to compute totals with AutoSum. AutoSum provides a convenient method for summing a range of numbers. However, you will need to use many other types of formulas in Excel. In fact, many worksheets, such as financial models, require hundreds or even thousands of complex formulas.

Beginning Character in Formulas

As you saw in the AutoSum discussion in the previous section, functions begin with an equals (=) sign. If you are typing a formula in a cell, it is recommended that you also begin it with an equals (=) sign, even though you can begin it with a plus (+) or a minus (–) sign. It is best to adopt one method in order to create consistency.

Cell and Range References

Formulas derive their power from the use of cell and range references. For example, in the previous exercise, you used AutoSum to insert the formula =SUM(B6:B10) in cell B11. Because the range reference (B6:B11) was used in the formula, you were able to copy the formula across the row using the fill handle. There are two important benefits to using references in formulas.

■ When references are used, formulas can be copied to other cells.

■ Since a reference refers to a cell or a range of cells, the formula results are automatically recalculated when the data is changed in the referenced cell(s).

The Language of Excel Formulas

Formulas can include the standard arithmetic operators shown in the following table. You can also use spaces within formulas to improve their appearance and readability. Notice that each formula in the table begins with an equals (=) sign. Also, keep in mind that each formula is entered into the same cell that displays the resulting calculation.

Please Excuse My Dear Aunt Sally

Excel formulas follow the algebraic hierarchy you learned about way back in middle or high school. This means that the formula completes operations in a specific order. You may have learned to memorize this hierarchy with the mnemonic "Please Excuse My Dear Aunt Sally":

Please-   Parentheses (grouping symbols)

Excuse-   Exponents

My-   Multiplication

Dear-   Division

Aunt-   Addition

Sally-   Subtraction

In order to control the order of operations, you can use parentheses to cause Excel to add before multiplying or subtract before dividing. Take a look at the following examples to see how the order of operations works with and without parentheses and how the resulting value will be different.

$=53+7*5=53+35=88$ Multiplication then addition

$=(53+7)*5=(60)*5=300$ Parentheses then multiplication

 Hands-On 3.2   Use the Keyboard to Create a Basic Formula

1. Click the Monthly Profit Projection sheet tab at the bottom of the Excel window.

2. Click cell B6.

3. Type **=B4*B17** in the cell, and then tap ⌷Enter⌷ to complete the formula.

4. Click cell B5.

5. Type **=b4/b19** in the cell, and then tap ⌷Enter⌷ to complete the formula.

Using Cell References in Formulas

A cell reference identifies which cell or range of cells contains the values to use in a formula. Cell references are one of three types: relative, absolute, or mixed. All formulas use the relative cell reference unless you specifically instruct Excel to use another type. You used relative cell references in the formulas you created in the last exercise. As this lesson continues, you will learn about the other two types of cell references.

Relative Cell References

A relative cell reference means the cell is *relative* to the cell that contains the formula. For example, when you create a formula in cell C3 to subtract A3 minus B3 (=A3–B3), Excel finds that the first value is two cells to the left of the formula. The second value is one cell to the left of the formula.

When you copy a formula, the cell references update automatically and refer to new cells relative to the new formula cell. For example, if you copied the formula mentioned in the previous paragraph down to cell C4, the new formula would be A4 minus B4 (=A4–B4). The first and second values are still relative to the same number of cells to the left of the formula cell.

	A	B	C	D	E	F
12	Total Costs	=SUM(B7:B10)	=SUM(C7:C10)	=SUM(D7:D10)	=SUM(E7:E10)	=SUM(F7:F10)
13	Gross Profit	=B6-B12	=C6-C12	=D6-D12	=E6-E12	=F6-F12

Notice that when a formula utilizing relative cell references in column B is copied through to column F, the cells referenced in the copied formulas will refer to cells relative to where they are pasted.

Point Mode

One potential danger that can occur when typing formulas is accidentally typing the incorrect cell reference. This is easy to do, especially if the worksheet is complex. Point mode can help you avoid this problem. With point mode, you can insert a cell reference in a formula by clicking the desired cell as you are typing the formula. Likewise, you can insert a range reference in a formula by dragging over the desired cells. You will use point mode in the next exercise.

Absolute Cell References

You have been using relative references thus far in this course. Relative references are convenient because they update automatically when formulas are moved or copied. In some situations, you may not want references updated when a formula is moved or copied. You must use absolute or mixed references in these situations. Absolute references always refer to the same cell, regardless of which cell the formula is moved or copied to. You can refer to cells on other worksheets or in other workbooks as well. In *FastCourse Excel 2007: Level 2*, you will learn about referring to cells in other locations.

Creating Absolute References

You create absolute references by placing dollar signs in front of the column and row components of the reference: for example, $C$1. You can type the dollar signs as you enter a formula or add them later by editing the formula. The following illustration shows an example of how absolute references are used in formulas.

	A	B	C	D	E	F
12	Total Costs	=SUM(B7:B10)	=SUM(C7:C10)	=SUM(D7:D10)	=SUM(E7:E10)	=SUM(F7:F10)
13	Gross Profit	=B6-B12	=C6-C12	=D6-D12	=E6-E12	=F6-F12
14	Net Profit	=B13*(1-$F$18)	=C13*(1-$F$18)	=D13*(1-$F$18)	=E13*(1-$F$18)	=F13*(1-$F$18)
15	Gross Profit vs. Revenue	=B13/B6	=C13/C6	=D13/D6	=E13/E6	=F13/F6

Cell B14 displays a formula that has both a relative cell reference (B13) and an absolute cell reference ($F$18).

When copied to cell C14, the relative cell reference will refer to the cell relative to where it is pasted (C13), but the absolute cell reference will remain the same.

Mixed References

You can mix relative and absolute references within a reference. For example, the reference $C1 is a combination of an absolute reference to column C and a relative reference to row 1. Mixed references are useful when copying many types of formulas.

Using the F4 Function Key

You make a reference absolute or mixed by typing dollar signs while entering the reference. You can also click in front of a reference in the Formula Bar and use the F4 function key to insert the dollar signs. The first time you tap F4, dollar signs are placed in front of both the column and row components of the reference. If you tap F4 again, the dollar sign is removed from the column component, thus creating a mixed reference. If you tap F4 a third time, a dollar sign is placed in front of just the column component and removed from the row component. One more tap of F4 will return you to a relative cell reference.

What-If Analysis

Another great advantage to using cell references in formulas is that it allows you to perform what-if analyses. A what-if analysis is as simple as changing the value in a cell that is referenced in a formula and observing the overall change in the data. You can perform these simple analyses at any time by replacing the value(s) in referenced cells. The Undo command can come in very handy when performing a what-if analysis as it provides a quick way to return the worksheet to the original values. If you wish to perform an extensive what-if analysis and not worry about losing your original data, you may wish to save your workbook under a different name as a "practice" file.

Hands-On 3.3 Create Formulas Using Cell References

1. Click cell B7, and type **=** to begin a formula.

2. Click cell B18, and then tap the F4 function key.

3. Type **+(** to continue the formula.

4. Click cell F19, and then tap F4.

5. Type *****, and then click cell B4.

6. Type **)**, and then click the Enter ✔ button to complete the formula.

7. Click cell B8, type **3500**, and then tap Enter to complete the entry.

8. Click cell B10, type **5000**, and then tap Enter.

9. Click the 1st Qtr Commissions tab.

10. Select the range B11:D11, and then look at the Status bar to determine the average number of commissionable nights booked per month.

11. Click the Monthly Profit Projection tab to return to that worksheet.

12. Click cell B9, and enter the formula **=1096*$B$17*$F$17** to calculate the commissions. Tap Enter to complete the entry.

13. Click cell B12, and choose Home→Editing→Sum **Σ** from the Ribbon.

14. Click and drag to select B7:B10 as the range, and then tap Enter.

15. Enter **=B6-B12** in cell B13, tapping Enter to complete the entry.

16. Enter **=B13*(1-$F$18)** in cell B14, tapping Enter to complete the entry.

17. Enter **=B13/B6** in cell B15, tapping Enter to complete the entry.

18. Take a look at the formulas displayed in the figure below to see how using absolute cell references differs from using relative cell references.

	A	B	C	D	E	F
4	Projected Nights Booked	=100*30	=125*30	=150*30	=175*30	=190*30
5	Occupancy Rate	=B4/$B$19	=C4/$B$19	=D4/$B$19	=E4/$B$19	=F4/$B$19
6	Revenue	=B4*$B$17	=C4*$B$17	=D4*$B$17	=E4*$B$17	=F4*$B$17
7	Operating Cost	=$B$18+($F$19*B4)	=$B$18+($F$19*C4)	=$B$18+($F$19*D4)	=$B$18+($F$19*E4)	=$B$18+($F$19*F4)
8	Advertising	3500	3500	3500	3500	3500
9	Commissions	=1096*$B$17*$F$17	=1096*$B$17*$F$17	=1096*$B$17*$F$17	=1096*$B$17*$F$17	=1096*$B$17*$F$17
10	Office Expenses	5000	5000	5000	5000	5000
11						
12	Total Costs	=SUM(B7:B10)	=SUM(C7:C10)	=SUM(D7:D10)	=SUM(E7:E10)	=SUM(F7:F10)
13	Gross Profit	=B6-B12	=C6-C12	=D6-D12	=E6-E12	=F6-F12
14	Net Profit	=B13*(1-$F$18)	=C13*(1-$F$18)	=D13*(1-$F$18)	=E13*(1-$F$18)	=F13*(1-$F$18)
15	Gross Profit vs. Revenue	=B13/B6	=C13/C6	=D13/D6	=E13/E6	=F13/F6
16						
17	Average Room Rate	89		Commission Rate		0.15
18	Monthly Fixed Operating Cost	200000		Tax Rate		0.25
19	Nights Per Month	=200*30		Variable Cost per Night		20

Modifying and Copying Formulas

You can modify and copy formulas in much the same way that you learned to edit and copy cells in the last lesson. We will use the tools learned previously and apply them to formulas in the next exercise.

Modifying Formulas

You can modify formulas in either the Formula Bar or the cell. If you select a cell and enter a new formula, it replaces the previous contents of the cell.

When you select a formula in order to edit it, you will see colored lines around all of the cells that are referenced by the formula. This can help you to visually determine if the formula is correct.

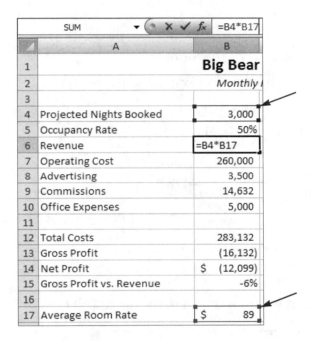

Notice that when the formula in B6 is selected for editing (as indicated by the insertion point in the Formula Bar), Excel will graphically display the cells that are being referenced by the formula, in this case cells B4 and B17.

Copying Formulas

You can use either the Copy and Paste commands with formulas or AutoFill in order to copy them to new cells. You can copy formulas to one cell at a time or to a range of cells using either method.

If you use AutoFill, the AutoFill Options button will appear once you have released the mouse button. Clicking this button will allow you to customize your fill.

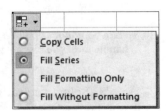

You can change what was copied in the cells through AutoFill by clicking the AutoFill Options button and choosing a different option.

Hands-On 3.4   Modify and Copy Formulas

1. Click cell B5, and enter **=B4/$B$19** to replace the current formula.

2. Click cell B6, and then follow these steps to edit the formula in the cell.

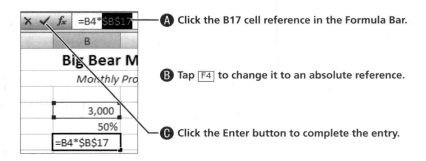

Ⓐ Click the B17 cell reference in the Formula Bar.

Ⓑ Tap F4 to change it to an absolute reference.

Ⓒ Click the Enter button to complete the entry.

3. Click cell B5, and then use Ctrl + C to copy the formula.

4. Click cell C5, and then use Ctrl + V to paste the formula in the new cell.

5. Select the range D5:F5, and then use Ctrl + V .

6. Click in cell D5, and look at the formula in the Formula Bar.

D5	▾	fx	=D4/$B$19	
	A	B	C	D
4	Projected Nights Booked	3,000	3,750	4,500
5	Occupancy Rate	50%	63%	75%

Notice that the relative cell reference now indicates cell D4, whereas the absolute cell reference is still looking to cell B19.

7. Follow these steps to copy the formula from cell B6 to the range C6:F6.

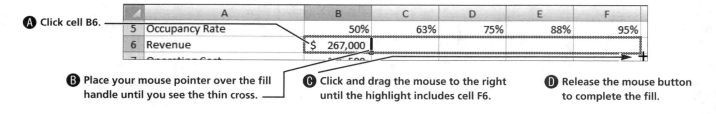

Ⓐ Click cell B6.

	A	B	C	D	E	F
5	Occupancy Rate	50%	63%	75%	88%	95%
6	Revenue	$ 267,000				

Ⓑ Place your mouse pointer over the fill handle until you see the thin cross.

Ⓒ Click and drag the mouse to the right until the highlight includes cell F6.

Ⓓ Release the mouse button to complete the fill.

8. Select the range B7:B15.

9. Place your mouse pointer over the fill handle at the bottom right of the selected range.

10. When you see the thin cross ➕, drag to the right until the highlight includes the cells in column F.

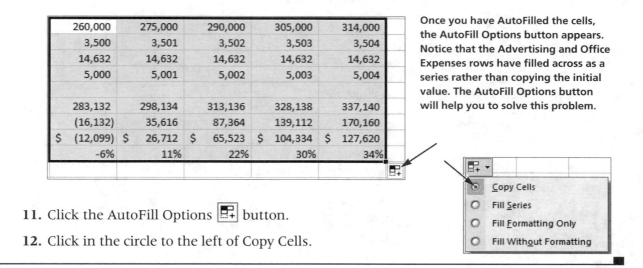

Once you have AutoFilled the cells, the AutoFill Options button appears. Notice that the Advertising and Office Expenses rows have filled across as a series rather than copying the initial value. The AutoFill Options button will help you to solve this problem.

11. Click the AutoFill Options ⊞ button.

12. Click in the circle to the left of Copy Cells.

Displaying Formulas

Excel normally displays the results of formulas in worksheet cells. However, you may need to display the actual formulas from time to time. Displaying the formulas can be helpful, especially in complex financial worksheets. Displaying formulas can help you understand how a worksheet functions. It can also be used to "debug" the worksheet and locate potential problems.

FROM THE KEYBOARD

Ctrl + ` to show formulas

To display formulas, you will use the Show Formulas button on the Formulas tab of the Ribbon. You can edit a formula in this view, but you will need to show values again to see the result. In order to view the values once again, click the Show Formulas button again.

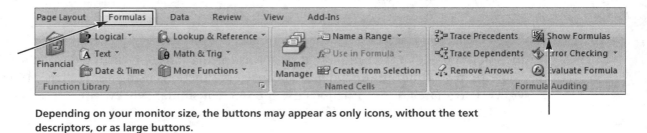

Depending on your monitor size, the buttons may appear as only icons, without the text descriptors, or as large buttons.

C	D	E
Big Bear Mountain Inn		
Monthly Projected Profits		
=125*30	=150*30	=175*30
=C4/$B$19	=D4/$B$19	=E4/$B$19
=C4*$B$17	=D4*$B$17	=E4*$B$17
=$B$18+($F$19*C4)	=$B$18+($F$19*D4)	=$B$18+($F$19*E4)
3500	3500	3500
=1096*$B$17*$F$17	=1096*$B$17*$F$17	=1096*$B$17*$F$17
5000	5000	5000
=SUM(C7:C10)	=SUM(D7:D10)	=SUM(E7:E10)
=C6-C12	=D6-D12	=E6-E12
=C13*(1-$F$18)	=D13*(1-$F$18)	=E13*(1-$F$18)
=C13/C6	=D13/D6	=E13/E6

When you choose to show formulas, you will see the formulas in the cells rather than the values as before. If a cell does not contain a formula, the contents will be visible in this view.

 Hands-On 3.5   Display Formulas in a Worksheet

1. Choose Formulas→Formula Auditing→Show Formulas from the Ribbon.

2. Choose Formulas→Formula Auditing→Show Formulas from the Ribbon.

Using Formula AutoComplete

 Excel 2007 includes a feature that serves to assist you in creating and editing formulas. Formula AutoComplete will jump into action once you have typed an equals (=) sign and the beginning letters of a function in a cell. It works by displaying a list of functions beginning with the typed letters below the active cell.

Functions Defined

A function is a predefined formula that performs calculations or returns a desired result. Excel has more than 400 built-in functions. You construct functions using a set of basic rules known as syntax. Fortunately, most functions use the same or similar syntax. This syntax also applies to the MIN, MAX, AVERAGE, and COUNT functions.

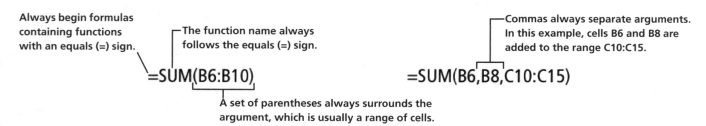

Always begin formulas containing functions with an equals (=) sign.

The function name always follows the equals (=) sign.

=SUM(B6:B10)

A set of parentheses always surrounds the argument, which is usually a range of cells.

Commas always separate arguments. In this example, cells B6 and B8 are added to the range C10:C15.

=SUM(B6,B8,C10:C15)

Hands-On 3.6   Use Formula AutoComplete

1. Display the 1st Qtr Commissions worksheet by clicking the sheet tab.

2. Click cell B12.

3. Type **=ave** and observe the list that results.

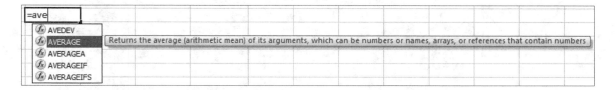

4. Double-click AVERAGE in the list.

5. Drag to select cells B6:B10 as the range for the formula.

6. Type **)** to complete the function, and then tap ⟨Enter⟩.

7. Click on cell B12, and use the fill handle to copy the function to the range of C12:E12.

11	Total	1116	1285	886	3287
12	Average	223.2	257	177.2	657.4
13	Maximum				

Using the Function Wizard

The Function Wizard f_x button displays the Insert Function dialog box. This dialog box provides access to all of Excel's built-in functions. It allows you to locate a function by typing a description or searching by category. When you locate the desired function and click OK, Excel displays the Function Arguments box. The Function Arguments box helps you enter arguments in functions. The Insert Function box and the Function Arguments box are shown in the following illustrations.

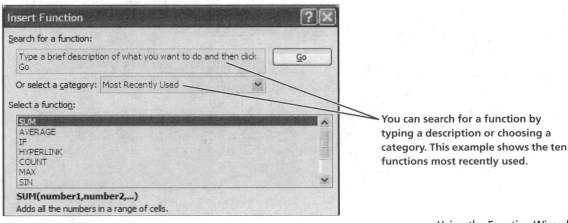

You can search for a function by typing a description or choosing a category. This example shows the ten functions most recently used.

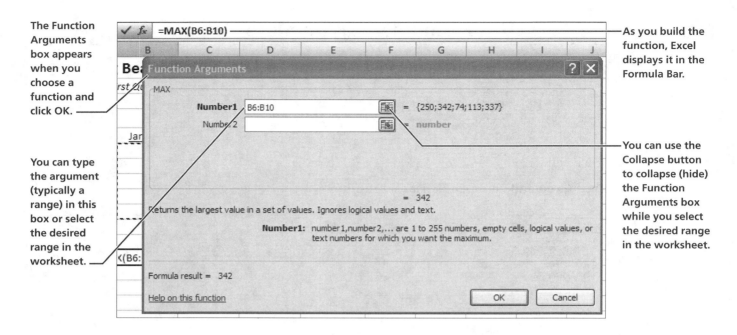

The Function Arguments box appears when you choose a function and click OK.

You can type the argument (typically a range) in this box or select the desired range in the worksheet.

✓ ƒx =MAX(B6:B10)

As you build the function, Excel displays it in the Formula Bar.

Function Arguments ? ✕

MAX

Number1 B6:B10 = {250;342;74;113;337}

Number2 = number

You can use the Collapse button to collapse (hide) the Function Arguments box while you select the desired range in the worksheet.

= 342

Returns the largest value in a set of values. Ignores logical values and text.

Number1: number1,number2,... are 1 to 255 numbers, empty cells, logical values, or text numbers for which you want the maximum.

Formula result = 342

Help on this function

OK | Cancel

Hands-On 3.7 Use the Function Wizard

1. Click in cell B13.

2. Follow these steps to create the Maximum function.

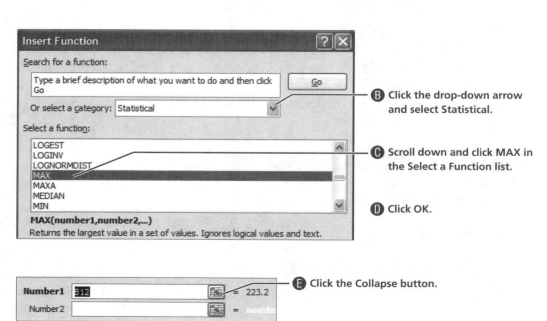

A Click the Function Wizard button.

	A	B
11	Total	1116
12	Average	223.2
13	Maximum	

Insert Function ? ✕

Search for a function:

Type a brief description of what you want to do and then click Go | Go

Or select a category: Statistical

B Click the drop-down arrow and select Statistical.

Select a function:

LOGEST
LOGINV
LOGNORMDIST
MAX
MAXA
MEDIAN
MIN

C Scroll down and click MAX in the Select a Function list.

D Click OK.

MAX(number1,number2,...)
Returns the largest value in a set of values. Ignores logical values and text.

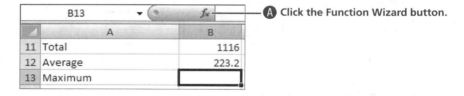

Number1 B12 = 223.2

Number2 = number

E Click the Collapse button.

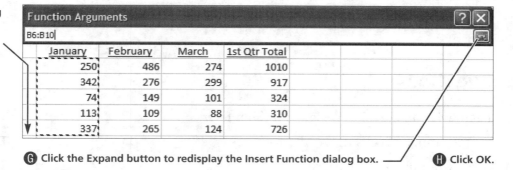

F Click and drag to select the range B6:B10.

Function Arguments

B6:B10

January	February	March	1st Qtr Total			
250	486	274	1010			
342	276	299	917			
74	149	101	324			
113	109	88	310			
337	265	124	726			

G Click the Expand button to redisplay the Insert Function dialog box. ——— **H** Click OK.

3. Use the fill handle to copy the formula to the range of C13:E13.

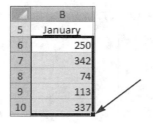

	B
5	January
6	250
7	342
8	74
9	113
10	337

If you recall, the fill handle is located at the bottom-right corner of the selection.

4. Using the steps outlined in step 2, create the Minimum function in cell B14.

5. Copy the function in cell B14 to the range of C14:E14.

6. Save your workbook and close Excel.

Concepts Review

True/False Questions

1. All formulas begin with an equals (=) sign or a cell reference.   TRUE   FALSE

2. AutoSum can total a range of cells that contains blanks.   TRUE   FALSE

3. MIN and MAX are examples of functions.   TRUE   FALSE

4. Function arguments are always surrounded by quotation marks (" ").   TRUE   FALSE

5. You can use more than one arithmetic operator in a formula.   TRUE   FALSE

6. When you type a cell reference in a formula, you must type the column letter   TRUE   FALSE
   in uppercase.

7. You use F4 to make a cell reference absolute.   TRUE   FALSE

8. You can use AutoFill to copy a formula.   TRUE   FALSE

9. Formula AutoComplete is the only way to sum a range of cells.   TRUE   FALSE

10. "Please Excuse Sally My Dear Aunt" is a way to remember the arithmetic order   TRUE   FALSE
    of operations.

Multiple Choice Questions

1. Which button launches the Function Wizard?
   a. AutoSum
   b. Insert Function
   c. Create Function
   d. AutoFunction

2. Which function calculates the highest value in a selection?
   a. COUNT
   b. MIN
   c. MAX
   d. AVERAGE

3. Which of the following statements about using AutoSum is true?
   a. AutoSum automatically sums a non-adjacent column or row of numbers.
   b. AutoSum automatically sums an adjacent column or row of numbers.
   c. AutoSum can sum only a list of values in the column above.
   d. None of the above

4. Which cell reference contains dollar signs?
   a. Absolute
   b. Relative
   c. Mixed
   d. Both a and c

LESSON 4

Formatting the Contents of Cells

In this lesson, you will learn how to use several of Excel's formatting features to enhance your worksheets. You will also learn powerful tools and techniques such as AutoFormat and the Format Painter. By the end of this lesson, you will have developed the skills necessary to produce professional-looking worksheets.

LESSON OBJECTIVES

After studying this lesson, you will be able to:

- Format worksheets using a variety of methods: Ribbon, Mini Toolbar, Format Cells Dialog Box
- Horizontally align and indent cell entries
- Apply and cancel text control options: merge, wrap text, and shrink to fit
- Format cell borders and fill colors
- Use the Format Painter tool to copy formatting
- Apply a theme to your worksheet
- Work with dates and create date and time functions

LESSON TIMING

- Concepts/Hands-On: 1 hr 00 min
- Concepts Review: 15 min
- Total: 1 hr 15 min

CASE STUDY: FORMATTING WITH EXCEL

Mendy Dobranski runs a computer and QuickBooks consulting business. She is working on her 3rd Quarter Income Statement for 2008. So far she has entered all of the data, but the report looks very drab and boring. She is now ready to spruce it up by using many of Excel's formatting features. Mendy will work to enhance the look of the text and numbers as well as cell characteristics such as the color displayed in the cells and the lines surrounding them.

Formatting Worksheets

Formatting deals with changing how the data in your worksheet looks, not with changing the data itself. In Excel and other Office programs, you can format text by changing the font, font size, and font color. You can also apply various font enhancements, including bold, italic, and underline. To format cells, select the desired cell(s) and apply formats using buttons on the Home tab of the Ribbon, by using the Format Cells dialog box, or by using the mini toolbar that appears when you right-click a cell or select text.

Formatting Entries with the Ribbon

The Font group on the Home tab of the Ribbon provides you with many popular formatting commands.

The Font group on the Home tab of the Ribbon makes finding formatting options easy.

Using the Mini Toolbar

The mini toolbar, a new feature in the Office 2007 Suite, will appear when text is selected. It will appear transparent until you move the mouse pointer over it. If you right-click a cell, the mini toolbar will appear non-transparent, ready to use. The mini toolbar will allow you to format the selected text without having to have the Home tab of the Ribbon displayed. This can be extremely convenient when you are primarily working with another tab of the Ribbon.

 **If you select text, the mini toolbar will appear transparent.**

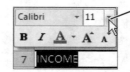 **Once the mouse pointer is placed over a cell or you right-click it, the mini toolbar will appear "solid."**

The mini toolbar will appear when text is selected, such as when "INCOME" is selected above.

Live Preview

In Office 2007, you will have the opportunity to preview how many formatting changes will look before actually issuing the command. Where this feature is available, you will see how the selected area will look when you place your mouse pointer over the formatting option.

FROM THE KEYBOARD
Ctrl+B for bold
Ctrl+I for italicize
Ctrl+U for underline

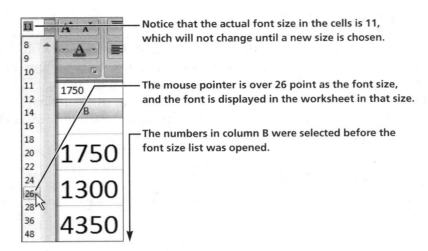

Notice that the actual font size in the cells is 11, which will not change until a new size is chosen.

The mouse pointer is over 26 point as the font size, and the font is displayed in the worksheet in that size.

The numbers in column B were selected before the font size list was opened.

 Hands-On 4.1   Format Cells with the Ribbon and Mini Toolbar

1. Start Excel.

2. Open the Mendy's Computer Services workbook in the Lesson 04 folder in your file storage location.

3. Follow these steps to change the font size for the entire worksheet:

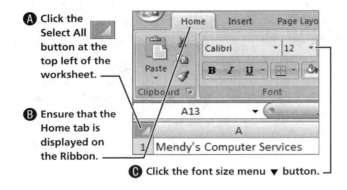

Ⓐ Click the Select All button at the top left of the worksheet.

Ⓑ Ensure that the Home tab is displayed on the Ribbon.

Ⓒ Click the font size menu ▼ button.

Ⓓ Choose 12.

4. Click cell A6.

5. Double-click the word *INCOME* in cell A6 two times—once to select the word, and once to open the mini toolbar.

6. Move the mouse pointer over the mini toolbar and click the Bold **B** button.

7. Right-click cell A12.

8. Click the Bold **B** button on the mini toolbar.

9. Use Ctrl+S to save your work before you move to the next topic.

Using Excel's Alignment and Indent Features

Excel allows you to alter how the text is aligned within cells. In addition to the standard left, center, right, and justify horizontal alignments, you can indent the contents within a cell from either edge.

Aligning Entries

The Align Left ![icon], Center ![icon], and Align Right ![icon] buttons on the Home tab of the Ribbon let you align entries within cells. By default, text entries are left aligned and number entries are right aligned. To change alignment, select the cell(s) and click the desired alignment button.

Indenting Cell Entries

The Increase Indent ![icon] button and Decrease Indent ![icon] button in the Alignment group on the Home tab of the Ribbon let you offset entries from the edges of cells. If a cell entry is left aligned, it will indent from the left edge, and if it is right aligned, it will indent from the right edge. Indenting is useful for conveying the hierarchy of entries. The following illustration shows indented cells:

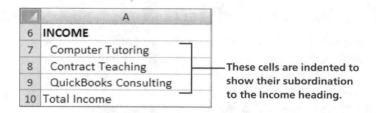

These cells are indented to show their subordination to the Income heading.

 Hands-On 4.2   Work with Alignment and Indent

1. Select the range B5:E5.

2. Choose Home→Alignment→Align Text Right ![icon] from the Ribbon.

3. Click cell A28.

4. Choose Home→Alignment→Align Text Right ![icon] from the Ribbon.

5. Follow these steps to indent entries in a range of cells:

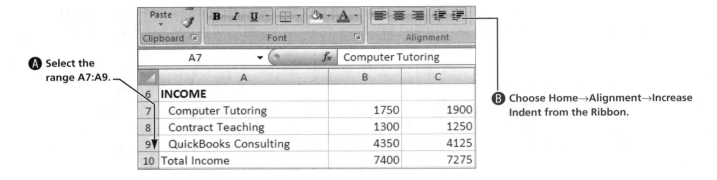

A Select the range A7:A9.

B Choose Home→Alignment→Increase Indent from the Ribbon.

6. Select the range A13:23.

7. Choose Home→Alignment→Increase Indent 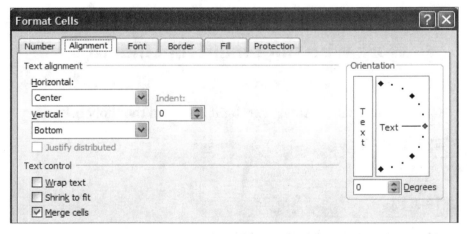 from the Ribbon.

Using Excel's Text Control Options

The Alignment tab of the Format Cells dialog box provides options that allow you to merge, wrap, and shrink cell entries. You can add multiple lines to a cell by inserting a line break or setting the Wrap Text option in the Format Cells dialog box.

You can control the alignment and whether cells are merged or split from the Alignment tab of the Format Cells dialog box.

Merging and Splitting Cells

Excel's Merge Cells option allows you to combine cells. Merged cells behave as one large cell, and you can merge cells vertically and horizontally. The merged cell takes on the name of the top left cell in the merged range. For example, if you merge cells A1:E1, the resulting merged cell will be named A1.

Merging Cells

The Merge Cells option is useful if you want to place a large block of text like a paragraph in the worksheet. You can merge cells by selecting the desired cells, clicking the Dialog Box Launcher button (as shown in the following figure) in the Alignment group on the Home tab of the Ribbon, and checking the Merge Cells box on the Alignment tab. Likewise, you can split a merged cell into the original cell configuration by removing the checkmark from the Merge Cells box.

Notice that the merged range is now named A1; essentially cells B1 to E1 do not exist as long as they are merged into A1.

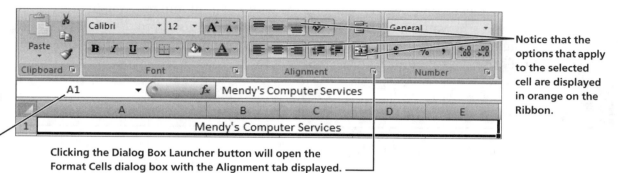

Notice that the options that apply to the selected cell are displayed in orange on the Ribbon.

Clicking the Dialog Box Launcher button will open the Format Cells dialog box with the Alignment tab displayed.

Merge & Center Command

The Merge & Center button merges selected cells and changes the alignment of the merged cell to center. This technique is often used to center a heading across columns. You split a merged and centered cell by clicking the Merge & Center button again. The Merge & Center menu button (see the following illustration) displays a menu with additional merge options.

The Merge & Center menu button

Clicking the menu ▼ button on the Merge & Center button results in a menu of merge and split options.

	A	B	C	D	E
1	Mendy's Computer Services				
2	Income Statement				
3	3rd Quarter 2008				

Cells A1:E1 are merged, and the Mendy's Computer Services heading is centered above columns A–E. The entire heading is contained within cell A1.

Wrapping Text

The Wrap Text option forces text to wrap within a cell as it would in a word processing document. You can turn the Wrap Text option on and off by selecting the desired cell(s), displaying the Alignment tab of the Format Cells dialog box, and checking or unchecking the Wrap Text box. You can also select the cells in which to wrap text and choose the Wrap Text button from the Home tab of the Ribbon.

Entering a Line Break

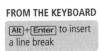

FROM THE KEYBOARD

Alt + Enter to insert a line break

You can add multiple lines to a cell by inserting a line break or setting the Wrap Text option in the Format Cells dialog box. Use the keystroke command Alt + Enter to insert a line break. To delete a line break, click to the right of the last word on the first line and tap Delete .

Shrinking Text to Fit Within a Cell

There may be times when changing the width of a column or wrapping text is not appropriate, yet you still want all of the text within the cell to be displayed. Excel has a feature on the Alignment tab of the Format Cells dialog box that allows you to shrink the cell entry to fit the cell "as is." This option is termed Shrink to Fit.

 Hands-On 4.3   Control Text in Cells

1. Select the range A1:E1.

2. Choose Home→Alignment→Merge & Center ⊞ from the Ribbon.

3. Click cell C1.

4. Select A2:E2.

5. Choose Home→Alignment→Merge & Center ⊞ from the Ribbon.

6. Repeat steps 4 and 5 for the range A3:E3.

7. Click cell E5.

8. Choose Home→Alignment→Wrap Text ⊞ from the Ribbon.

9. use Ctrl + Z to undo the last command.

10. Follow these steps to manually enter a line break in the cell:

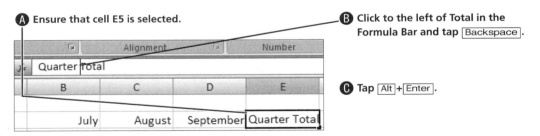

Ⓐ Ensure that cell E5 is selected.

Ⓑ Click to the left of Total in the Formula Bar and tap Backspace .

Ⓒ Tap Alt + Enter .

11. Tap Enter to complete the entry.

12. Use Ctrl + S to save your work.

Formatting Numbers

Excel lets you format numbers in a variety of ways. Number formats change the way numbers are displayed, though they do not change the actual numbers. Once a number formatting has been applied to a cell, it remains with the cell—even if the contents are deleted. The following table describes the most common number formats.

Number Format	Description
General	Numbers are formatted with the General Style format by default. It does not apply any special formats to the numbers.
Comma	The Comma Style format inserts a comma after every third digit in the number. It also inserts a decimal point and two decimal places, which can be removed if desired.
Currency	The Currency Style format is the same as the Comma format except that it adds a dollar ($) sign in front of the number.
Percent	A percent (%) sign is inserted to the right of the number in the Percent Style. The percentage is calculated by multiplying the number by 100.

Using the Number Command Group

The Number Command group on the Home tab of the Ribbon allows you to format your numbers in a variety of ways, with the most common styles displayed as buttons. The top area of the group displays the number formatting of the selected cell(s). Clicking the menu button to the right of the current number formatting displays a menu of additional number format options.

If you click the Dialog Box Launcher button in the Number group, the Format Cells dialog box will appear with the Number tab displayed.

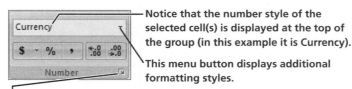

Notice that the number style of the selected cell(s) is displayed at the top of the group (in this example it is Currency).

This menu button displays additional formatting styles.

Clicking the Dialog Box Launcher button will open the Format Cells dialog box with the Number tab selected.

Using Accounting and Currency Styles

There are two number styles that apply currency symbols (such as dollar signs) to numbers. You will notice a difference in where the dollar sign is placed based on the style you select. If you choose the accounting style, currency symbols will appear fixed at the left of the cells. The currency style, on the other hand, will display the currency symbol next to the number in the cell.

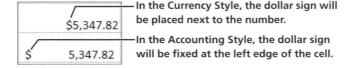

In the Currency Style, the dollar sign will be placed next to the number.

In the Accounting Style, the dollar sign will be fixed at the left edge of the cell.

Applying the Percent Style

In the Hands-On exercise from the previous lesson, cells were formatted with the Percent Style for you. This should reinforce the idea that once you apply formatting to a cell, it will remain until you change or clear it, regardless of whether there is any data contained in the cell. In order to apply the Percent Style yourself, you have two options.

- Select the cells that you wish to format as Percent Style and apply the formatting. If you format the cells first, you can type 25 and it will be formatted as 25%.

- Type the value in the cell first, and then apply the Percent Style formatting. If you type in the value first, you will need to type it in as a decimal. For instance, you will need to type in .25 in order for it to format properly as 25%. If you type in 25 and then apply Percent Style formatting, it will appear as 2500%.

Displaying Negative Numbers

Negative number displays can be either preceded by a minus sign or surrounded by parentheses. You can also display negative numbers in red. The Currency option and Number option in the Format Cells dialog box let you choose the format for negative numbers.

The negative number format you choose affects the alignment of numbers in the cells. If the format displays negative numbers in parentheses, a small space equal to the width of a closing parenthesis appears on the right edge of cells containing positive numbers. Excel does this so the decimal points are aligned in columns containing both positive and negative numbers.

16	Internet	45	45
17	Professional Dues	0	500
18	Rent	1500	1500
19	Software	-50	0
20	Subscriptions	25	0

When the numbers are formatted as General Style, the negative numbers will be displayed with a minus sign in front of them.

16	Internet	45.00	45.00
17	Professional Dues	-	500.00
18	Rent	1,500.00	1,500.00
19	Software	(50.00)	-
20	Subscriptions	25.00	-

When you choose the Comma Style format, you can accept the default negative number format with parentheses or change it to display a minus sign in the Format Cells dialog box. If you choose to format negative numbers with parentheses, the positive numbers will be set a bit further from the right edge of the cell in order for the decimal points to be aligned. Notice also that the cells containing the number 0 are displayed with dashes.

Hands-On 4.4   Format Numbers

1. Follow these steps to apply Currency Style format to a range of cells:

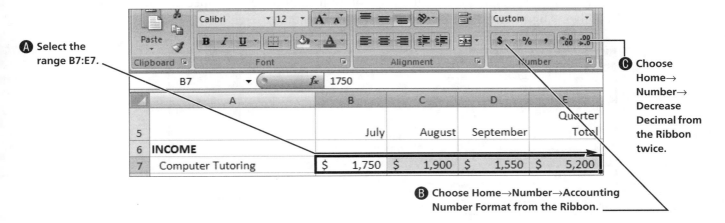

A Select the range B7:E7.

B Choose Home→Number→Accounting Number Format from the Ribbon.

C Choose Home→ Number→ Decrease Decimal from the Ribbon twice.

2. Select the range B8:E9.

3. Choose Home→Number→Comma Style ▪ from the Ribbon.

4. Choose Home→ Number→Decrease Decimal .00 from the Ribbon twice.

5. Select the range B10:E10, hold down Ctrl, and select the range B24:E25.

6. Choose Home→Accounting Number Format $ from the Ribbon.

7. Choose Home→Decrease Decimal .00 from the Ribbon twice.

8. Select the range B13:E23.

9. Apply Comma Style formatting with no decimals to the selection.

10. Use Ctrl + S to save your work.

Using the Format Cells Dialog Box

We have discussed the Number and Alignment tabs of the Format Cells dialog box; now we will examine in more depth how to truly utilize this important dialog box. There are six tabs in the Format Cells dialog box that allow you to format different aspects of your worksheet: Number, Alignment, Font, Border, Fill, and Protection.

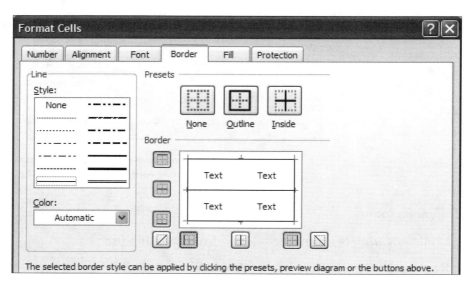

The Border tab of the Format Cells dialog box allows you to set the borders for the selected cells. In this example, a line will appear around the entire selection as well as between each row that is selected.

Borders and Fill Color

The Borders ⊞▾ button on the Home tab of the Ribbon lets you add borders to cell edges. When you click the Borders menu ▾ button, a list of options appears. You can apply a border style to all selected cells by choosing it from the list. You can also choose More Borders from the bottom of the list to display the Borders tab of the Format Cells dialog box.

The image displayed on the Borders button on the Ribbon will change based on the last border applied. This feature makes it easy to apply the same border formatting throughout the workbook.

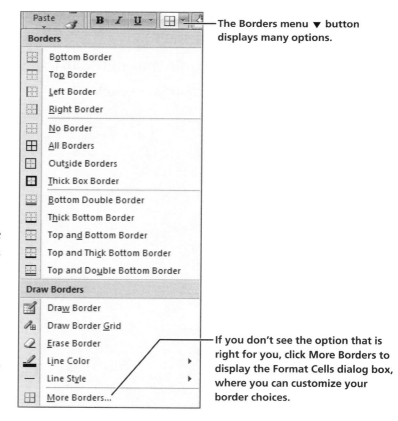

The Borders menu ▾ button displays many options.

If you don't see the option that is right for you, click More Borders to display the Format Cells dialog box, where you can customize your border choices.

Applying Fill Colors and Patterns

The Fill Color button on the Home tab of the Ribbon lets you fill the background of selected cells with color. When you click the Fill Color menu button, a palette of colors appears. You can apply a color to all selected cells by choosing it from the palette. The fill color is independent of the font color used to format text and numbers. The Format Cells dialog box has a Fill tab that lets you apply fill colors and a variety of patterns and effects.

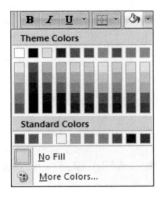

This palette of colors results when you click the Fill Color menu ▼ button. The color you choose will fill the cell but will not affect the color of the font.

Hands-On 4.5   Format with the Format Cells Dialog Box

1. Select the range A1:E25.

2. Choose Home→Font→Borders menu ▼→More Borders from the Ribbon.

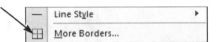

3. Follow these steps to apply the border formatting:

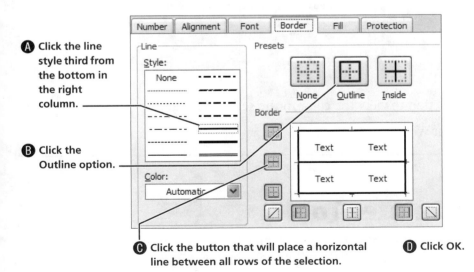

Ⓐ Click the line style third from the bottom in the right column.

Ⓑ Click the Outline option.

Ⓒ Click the button that will place a horizontal line between all rows of the selection.

Ⓓ Click OK.

4. Use Ctrl + Z to undo the borders.

5. Select the range B9:E9, hold down the Ctrl key, and select the range B23:E23. Then release the Ctrl key.

6. Click the Borders menu ▼ button.

7. Choose the Bottom Border option to place a border along the bottom of the selected cells.

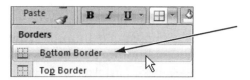

8. Select the range B25:E25.

9. Click the Borders button drop-down arrow, and choose Top and Double Bottom Border.

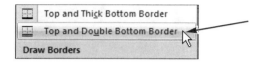

10. Select the range A6:E6, hold down the ⟨Ctrl⟩ key, and select A12:E12. Then release the ⟨Ctrl⟩ key.

11. Follow these steps to apply a fill color to the selected ranges:

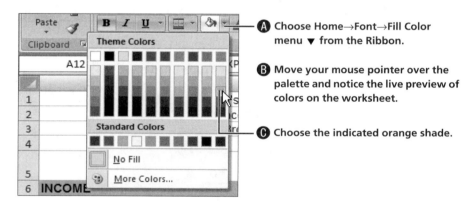

Ⓐ Choose Home→Font→Fill Color menu ▼ from the Ribbon.

Ⓑ Move your mouse pointer over the palette and notice the live preview of colors on the worksheet.

Ⓒ Choose the indicated orange shade.

12. Click away from the selection to view the color in the selected ranges.

13. Use ⟨Ctrl⟩+⟨S⟩ to save your work.

Using the Format Painter Tool

There may be times when you want to copy the formatting from one cell to another without copying the contents. The Format Painter lets you copy text formats and number formats from one cell to another. This tool can be extremely helpful if you have a cell to which many formatting options have been applied and you do not wish to apply each option individually to another cell or range of cells.

Hands-On 4.6   Copy Formatting with Format Painter

1. Click cell A12.

2. Choose Home→Clipboard→Format Painter button from the Ribbon.

3. Select the range A25:E25.

4. Choose Home→Number→Accounting Number Format **$** from the Ribbon.

5. Choose Home→Number→Decrease Decimal from the Ribbon twice.

Formatting with Themes

2007 new! Themes allow you to easily apply formatting to your entire worksheet. The themes provided in Excel have been developed by designers at Microsoft and help you to choose fonts, styles, and colors that match nicely.

There is good advice that you should heed when using different font styles—do not use too many of them on one worksheet. You can "overformat" your worksheet! Themes allow you to choose matching fonts and styles if you are design-challenged.

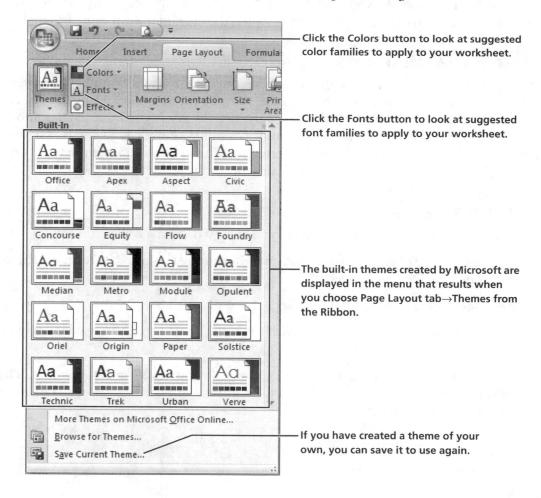

Click the Colors button to look at suggested color families to apply to your worksheet.

Click the Fonts button to look at suggested font families to apply to your worksheet.

The built-in themes created by Microsoft are displayed in the menu that results when you choose Page Layout tab→Themes from the Ribbon.

If you have created a theme of your own, you can save it to use again.

Hands-On 4.7   Apply a Theme to a Worksheet

1. Select the range A1:E25.

2. Choose Page Layout →Themes→Themes from the Ribbon.

3. Choose the Apex theme.

4. Practice applying themes until you find one that suits you.

Inserting Date Functions and Formatting

In the previous lesson, we explored a variety of statistical functions. Now we will insert a function that will always display today's date. Excel will determine the date to display according to your computer's clock feature.

Working with Dates

Dates are used in workbooks in two ways. First, you can simply display dates in cells using various formats such as 12/25/07; December 25, 2007; or 25-Dec-07. Second, you can use dates in formulas. For example, you may want to compute the number of days an invoice is past due. You calculate this as the difference between the current date and the original invoice date.

Date Serial Numbers

When you enter a date in a cell, Excel converts the date to a serial number between 1 and 2,958,525. These numbers correspond to the 10-millennium period from January 1, 1900, through December 31, 9999. The date January 1, 1900, is assigned the serial number 1; January 2, 1900, is assigned the serial number 2; and December 31, 9999, is assigned the serial number 2,958,525. When dates are converted to numbers, you can use the numbers/dates in calculations. Best of all, it's done for you automatically!

Entering Dates

Excel performs the following steps when you enter a date in a cell:

■ It recognizes the entry as a date if you enter it using a standard date format such as 12/25/07; December 25, 2007; or 25-Dec-07.

■ It converts the date to a serial number between 1 and 2,958,525.

■ It formats the serial number entry with the same date format you used when you entered the date.

This roundabout process occurs behind the scenes so you never see it happening. The benefit of converting dates to numbers and then formatting them with a date format is that the dates can be used in calculations.

Inserting Date and Time Functions

In Lesson 3, Working with Formulas and Functions, you learned about some of Excel's powerful statistical functions. In *FastCourse Excel 2007: Level 3*, you will learn about financial and database functions. In this lesson, you will see the value of using date and time functions in Excel.

About Date Functions

The current date is often required in worksheets. You may also want to show the date the worksheet was created or printed. The following details apply in general to dates you insert with date functions:

- You can insert a date function rather than typing the date in a worksheet.

- Date functions produce the current date and, depending on the specific function, can update automatically.

- You insert date functions with the Insert Function dialog box or by typing the function in the result cell.

- Date functions are not case sensitive so you can type the formula in lowercase.

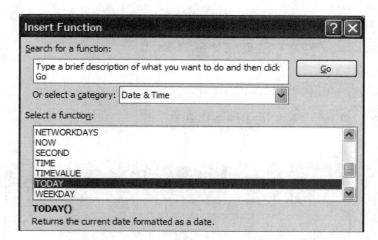

In the Date & Time function category, Excel provides a variety of functions. Notice that there is a description of the selected function displayed below the list.

1. Click cell B28.

2. Type **9/1/07** in the cell, and then click Enter ✓ on the Formula Bar.

3. Display the Home tab of the Ribbon.

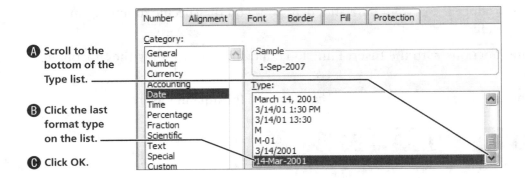

4. Click the Dialog Box Launcher ▣ in the Number group of the Home tab.

5. Follow these steps to change the date format:

Ⓐ Scroll to the bottom of the Type list.

Ⓑ Click the last format type on the list.

Ⓒ Click OK.

Number	Alignment	Font	Border	Fill	Protection

Category:
General
Number
Currency
Accounting
Date
Time
Percentage
Fraction
Scientific
Text
Special
Custom

Sample
1-Sep-2007

Type:
March 14, 2001
3/14/01 1:30 PM
3/14/01 13:30
M
M-01
3/14/2001
14-Mar-2001

6. Ensure that cell B28 is still selected, and then tap ⌐Delete⌐.

7. Follow these steps to enter the TODAY function:

Ⓐ Click the Insert Function button.

Ⓑ Choose Date & Time as the category.

Ⓒ Scroll down until TODAY is visible.

Ⓓ Double-click TODAY.

Ⓔ Click OK in the Function Argument dialog box.

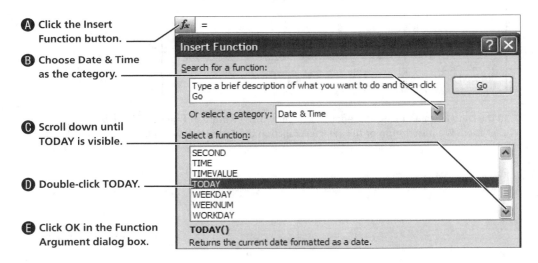

fx =

Insert Function

Search for a function:

Type a brief description of what you want to do and then click Go   Go

Or select a category: Date & Time

Select a function:

SECOND
TIME
TIMEVALUE
TODAY
WEEKDAY
WEEKNUM
WORKDAY

TODAY()
Returns the current date formatted as a date.

8. Use ⌐Ctrl⌐+⌐S⌐ to save your work.

9. Close ⌐×⌐ Excel.

Concepts Review

True/False Questions

1. When you choose to fill a cell with color, it will automatically change the font color to one that complements it.   TRUE   FALSE

2. The Merge & Center command can be used only with numbers.   TRUE   FALSE

3. The Comma Style inserts a dollar sign in front of numbers.   TRUE   FALSE

4. The Format Painter copies text formats but not number formats.   TRUE   FALSE

5. You can change a font's style and size but not its color.   TRUE   FALSE

6. You can use a keyboard command to force a line break and text wrapping in a cell.   TRUE   FALSE

7. Formats cannot be copied.   TRUE   FALSE

8. By double-clicking the Format Painter button, you can copy formats into multiple locations.   TRUE   FALSE

9. Titles can be centered across multiple columns.   TRUE   FALSE

10. Dates are not able to be used in formulas and functions.   TRUE   FALSE

Multiple Choice Questions

1. Which feature allows you to easily apply formatting when the Home tab of the Ribbon is not displayed?
   a. Mini toolbar
   b. Quick Access toolbar
   c. Live Preview
   d. None of the above

2. What must you do before clicking the Merge & Center button?
   a. Click the cell that contains the entry you wish to center.
   b. Select the cells you wish to center the entry across, making sure the entry is included in the selection.
   c. Select the entire row that contains the entry you wish to merge.
   d. None of the above

3. What keyboard command creates a line break within a cell?
   a. Alt + Enter
   b. Ctrl + Shift
   c. Alt + Shift
   d. Ctrl + Enter

4. Which function displays the current system date and time and calculates the serial number?
   a. =TODAY ( )
   b. =TODAY'S DATE ( )
   c. =DATE ( )
   d. =NOW ( )

LESSON 5

Changing the Appearance of Worksheets

In this lesson, you will learn techniques for changing the structure of worksheets as it relates to rows, columns, and additional cell alignment options. In addition, you will learn about a variety of Excel's tools such as the Spelling tool and features such as Find and Replace. After you complete this lesson, you will have all of the basics you need to work with Excel.

LESSON OBJECTIVES

After studying this lesson, you will be able to:

- Modify column width and row height
- Insert as well as delete columns, rows, and cells
- Hide and unhide rows and columns
- Set the vertical alignment and rotate the text
- Find data in a worksheet and replace both data and formatting
- Effectively utilize AutoCorrect
- Search Help to learn how to complete a task
- Work with Excel tools: Spelling, Research, Thesaurus, and Translation

LESSON TIMING

- Concepts/Hands-On: 1 hr 15 min
- Concepts Review: 15 min
- Total: 1 hr 30 min

CASE STUDY: CREATING MR. FITZPATRICK'S TEST BLUEPRINT

Mr. Fitzpatrick is creating a test blueprint in order to ensure that the test he is about to create for Lesson 3, Working with Formulas and Functions, is aligned to the learning objectives in the lesson. The blueprint includes a content outline that lists the learning objectives, Bloom's Taxonomy categories (which delineate the levels of complexity of the questions), an area where the number of test items is recorded, and Total and Percentage columns. You will be working with the structure of the worksheet, finding and replacing text and formats, working with vertical alignment and rotation, and utilizing Excel's proofing tools such as the spelling checker to finalize the worksheet.

Modifying Columns and Rows

As you have seen, many entries do not fit within the default column size. Worksheets can also appear overcrowded with the standard row heights, which may tempt you to insert blank rows to make the worksheet more readable. The problem with this "fix," though, is that it can cause problems down the road when you begin to use some of Excel's more powerful features. In this lesson, you will use more time-saving techniques to fix column width and row height issues, such as changing multiple columns and rows at the same time and using AutoFit to let Excel figure out the best width or height. Both of these commands simply require you to select multiple columns or rows before issuing the command.

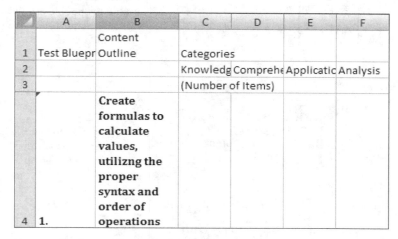

You can see that we have a lot of work to do here in resizing rows and columns!

Column Widths and Row Heights

There are a variety of methods for changing widths of columns and heights of rows. They can be performed on either one or multiple columns or rows. Probably the most efficient way to adjust widths and heights is to simply drag the heading lines of the column(s) or row(s).

Standard Column Widths and Row Heights

Each column in a new worksheet has a standard width of 8.43 characters, where the default character is Calibri 11 point. Each row has a standard height of 15 points, which is approximately one-fifth of an inch.

AutoFit

You can adjust both column widths and row heights with the AutoFit command. AutoFit adjusts column widths to fit the widest entry in a column. Likewise, AutoFit adjusts row heights to accommodate the tallest entry in a row. The following Quick Reference table discusses AutoFit options and other commands for setting column widths and row heights.

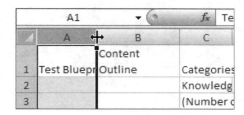

When you point to the border between columns or rows, a double-pointed arrow lets you know you can manually drag to change its size or double-click to issue the AutoFit command.

Hands-On 5.1   **Change Column Width and Row Height**

1. Open the Mr. Fitzpatrick's Content Outline file from the Lesson 05 folder in your file storage location.

2. Follow these steps to resize column A:

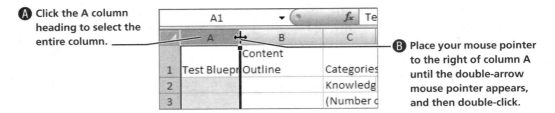

Ⓐ Click the A column heading to select the entire column.

Ⓑ Place your mouse pointer to the right of column A until the double-arrow mouse pointer appears, and then double-click.

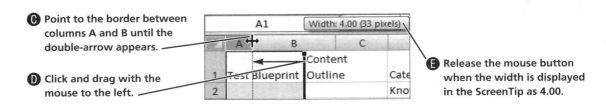

Ⓒ Point to the border between columns A and B until the double-arrow appears.

Ⓓ Click and drag with the mouse to the left.

Ⓔ Release the mouse button when the width is displayed in the ScreenTip as 4.00.

3. Click the column B header to select the entire column.

4. Follow these steps to precisely set the column width:

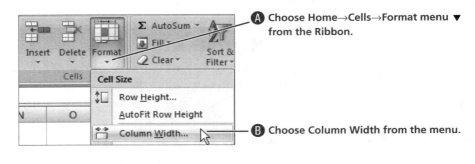

Ⓐ Choose Home→Cells→Format menu ▼ from the Ribbon.

Ⓑ Choose Column Width from the menu.

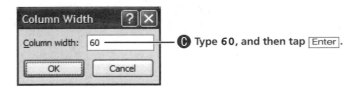

Ⓒ Type 60, and then tap ⎯Enter⎯.

5. Click the header for row 4, and then drag down through row 23.

6. Choose Home→Cells→Format menu ▼→AutoFit Row Height from the Ribbon as shown.

7. Use ⎯Ctrl⎯+⎯S⎯ to save your work.

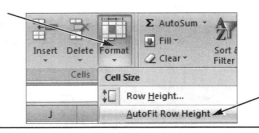

Inserting and Deleting Columns, Rows, and Cells

You can insert and delete columns, rows, and cells as needed in your worksheets. You probably figure that you will have plenty of rows and columns since you start out with more than 1,000,000 and 16,000 of them, respectively. The ability to insert and delete will come in handy when you want to restructure your worksheet after it has been created.

Inserting and Deleting Rows and Columns

Excel lets you insert and delete rows and columns. This gives you the flexibility to restructure your worksheets after they have been set up. The Quick Reference table in this section discusses the various procedures used to insert and delete rows and columns.

Inserting and Deleting Cells

If you want to insert or delete only cells, not entire rows or columns, you need to issue a command to insert or delete cells. This will allow you to add or remove a "chunk" or range of cells from your worksheet. This may cause problems because it alters the structure of your entire worksheet. For this reason, use this feature cautiously.

Shift Cells Option

When you add or remove a range of cells from your worksheet, you will need to tell Excel how to shift the surrounding cells to either make room for the addition or fill the space from the deletion.

The Appearance of the Cells Group Commands

The buttons in the Cells group of the Home tab of the Ribbon will appear differently depending on the size of your Excel window (which may be determined by the size of your monitor).

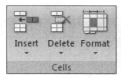

The figure on the left displays how the Cells group buttons will be displayed in a larger window, whereas the figure on the right displays the buttons as displayed in a smaller window. In the exercise steps, you will see the illustrations depicting the larger Ribbon buttons.

 Hands-On 5.2   Add and Remove Rows, Columns, and Cells

1. Select rows 15 and 23, using the [Ctrl] key to select nonadjacent rows.

2. Choose Home→Cells→Delete menu ▼→Delete Sheet Rows from the Ribbon.

3. Select row 8.

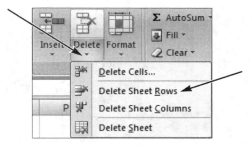

4. Point (don't click) over the Home→Cells→Insert 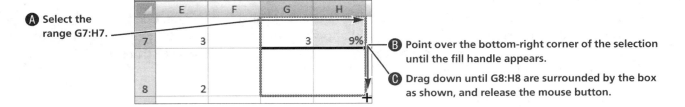 button on the Ribbon as shown.

5. Click the Insert button (not the menu ▼ button).

6. Enter the text in the following illustration into the appropriate cells.

	A	B	C	D	E
8	d.	The student will demonstrate how to use functions on the status bar in order to determine the minimum and maximum values in a range of cells.			2

7. Follow these steps to copy the necessary formulas:

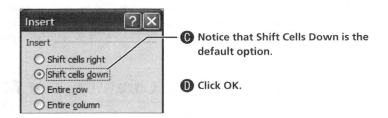

Ⓐ Select the range G7:H7.

Ⓑ Point over the bottom-right corner of the selection until the fill handle appears.

Ⓒ Drag down until G8:H8 are surrounded by the box as shown, and release the mouse button.

8. Select the range B1:H1.

9. Follow these steps to insert the cells and shift your existing data down:

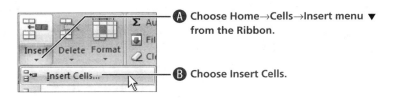

Ⓐ Choose Home→Cells→Insert menu ▼ from the Ribbon.

Ⓑ Choose Insert Cells.

Ⓒ Notice that Shift Cells Down is the default option.

Ⓓ Click OK.

10. Select cell A3.

11. Choose Home→Cells→Insert from the Ribbon.

12. Select row 1.

13. Choose Home→Cells→Insert from the Ribbon again.

14. Follow these steps to merge and center a range:

■ Select the range A1:H1.

■ Choose Home→Alignment→Merge & Center from the Ribbon.

15. Merge & Center ⊞ A2:H2, and then change the font size to 20.

16. Move (cut and paste) the contents of B3 to A3, and then merge and center ⊞ A3:B3.

17. Select B3:B4, and then click the Merge & Center ⊞ button twice.

18. Merge and center ⊞ C3:H3, and then place a border along the bottom of the cells.

19. Merge and center ⊞ C5:G5.

20. Right-align ≣ B25:B26.

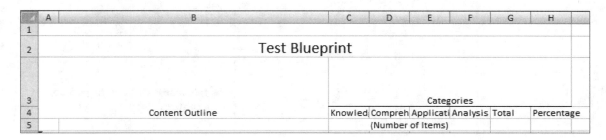

21. Use Ctrl + S to save your work.

Hiding Columns and Rows

There may be times when you wish to hide certain rows or columns from view. The hidden rows and columns will not be visible, nor will they print. However, the hidden rows and columns will still be part of the worksheet, and their values and formulas could still be referenced by other formulas in the visible rows and columns. Hiding rows and columns can be useful when you want to focus attention on other parts of the worksheet.

Notice that column F and row 1 are not visible once the Hide command is issued.

Unhiding Columns and Rows

After rows or columns have been hidden, you must issue an Unhide command to make them visible once again. Before the command to unhide rows is issued, you must select at least one row above and one row below the hidden ones. Likewise, you must select at least one column to the left and one to the right of the hidden ones before issuing the Unhide command. If you have hidden column A or row 1, you will need to drag to select from row 2 up to the column headers or from column B left through the row headers.

1. Follow these steps to hide column F:

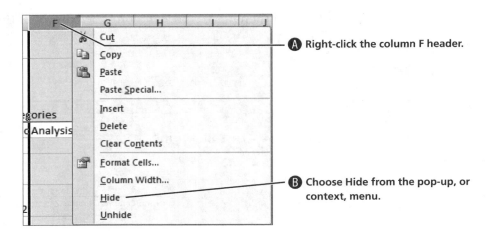

A Right-click the column F header.

B Choose Hide from the pop-up, or context, menu.

2. Right-click the row 1 header, and then choose Hide from the context menu.

3. Follow these steps to unhide column F:

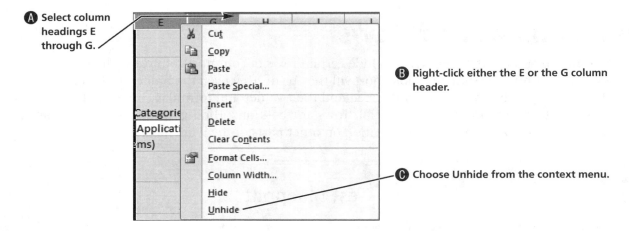

A Select column headings E through G.

B Right-click either the E or the G column header.

C Choose Unhide from the context menu.

4. Follow these steps to unhide row 1:

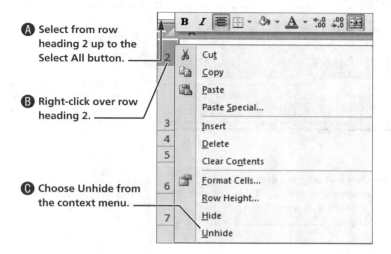

Ⓐ Select from row heading 2 up to the Select All button.

Ⓑ Right-click over row heading 2.

Ⓒ Choose Unhide from the context menu.

5. Use Ctrl + S to save your work.

Changing Vertical Alignment and Rotating Text

You have already learned many techniques for arranging data. Now you will be expanding on that knowledge and learning how to change the vertical alignment and rotate the contents of cells.

Setting Vertical Alignment

In the previous lesson, you learned how to align the contents of cells horizontally. This lesson will focus on vertical alignment within cells. Vertical alignment options include top, bottom, center, and justify. The default alignment is bottom. The Justify option is useful with multiple-line entries. For example, the Justify option evenly distributes unused space between lines in a multiple-line entry. Vertical alignment is set by choosing the Dialog Box Launcher button in the Alignment group on the Home tab of the Ribbon. You can also set top, bottom, and middle vertical alignment via buttons on the Ribbon.

Rotating Text

Text can be rotated from 0 to 90 degrees using the Orientation option on the Alignment tab in the Format Cells dialog box. Excel automatically increases the row height to accommodate the rotated text. When column headings are extra wide, making the worksheet spread out too far horizontally, you might consider rotating the text to save room. It can also be used for aesthetic purposes as it can spice up the appearance of a worksheet.

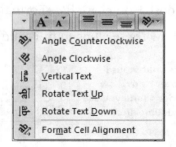

Excel has several preset rotations available on the Ribbon that you can apply to text in a cell.

Hands-On 5.4   Change Text's Vertical Alignment and Rotation

1. Follow these steps to rotate text:

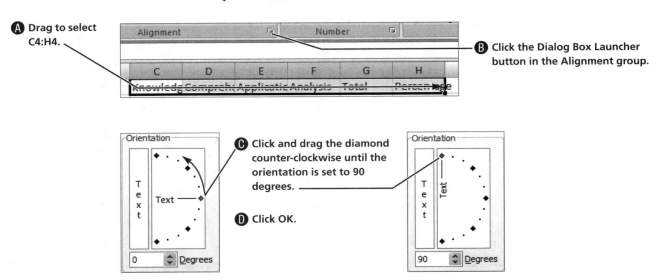

2. Follow these steps to AutoFit columns C through H:

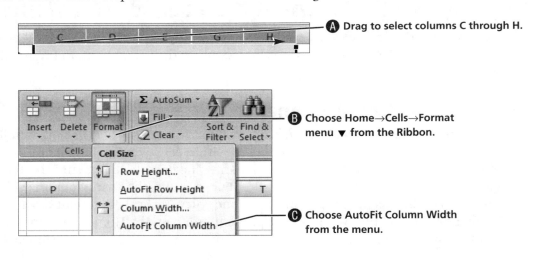

3. Select the row headings for rows 3 and 4.

4. Choose Home→Cells→Format menu ▼→AutoFit Row Height from the Ribbon.

5. Follow these steps to finish adjusting the row height for row 4:

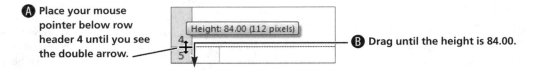

6. Select cell A3.

7. Choose Home→Alignment→Middle Align ≡ from the Ribbon.

8. Set the font size of cell A3 to 16.

9. Use $\boxed{\text{Ctrl}} + \boxed{\text{S}}$ to save your work.

Using Excel's Find and Replace Command

Excel's Find command performs searches on a worksheet or an entire workbook. It can search for a particular word, number, cell reference, formula, or format. Find is often the quickest way to locate an item in a workbook. The Replace feature helps you to find an item and replace it with a specified item.

Replacing Cell Formats

Excel lets you find and replace not just text but also cell formats. For example, you may want to search all worksheets and workbooks for cells formatted with Currency Style with no decimals and replace that format with Currency Style with two decimals. Finding and replacing cell formats can be a big time-saver, especially with large worksheets and multiple-sheet workbooks.

FROM THE KEYBOARD
$\boxed{\text{Ctrl}} + \boxed{\text{F}}$ to find
$\boxed{\text{Ctrl}} + \boxed{\text{H}}$ to replace

You can limit the Find and Replace command to specific areas of a workbook.

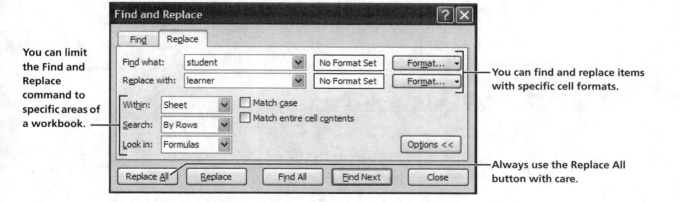

You can find and replace items with specific cell formats.

Always use the Replace All button with care.

Hands-On 5.5   Find and Replace Entries

1. Choose Home→Editing→Find & Select  →Replace from the Ribbon.

2. Follow these steps to prepare to replace all instances of *student* with *learner*:

A Type **student** in the Find What field.

B Tap [Tab], and then type **learner** in the Replace With field.

C Click Find Next to see the next place that *student* appears in your worksheet.

D Click Replace to replace just this one instance of *student*.

E Click Replace All to replace every instance of *student* in the worksheet.

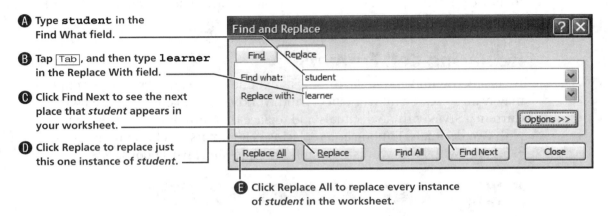

3. Click OK to acknowledge the total number of replacements.

4. Click the Options button in the Find and Replace dialog box.

5. Follow these steps to set the formatting to find:

A Delete the contents of the Find What box.

B Delete the contents of the Replace With box.

C Click the drop-down arrow on the top Format button.

D Choose the Choose Format From Cell option.

E Click to select cell B6.

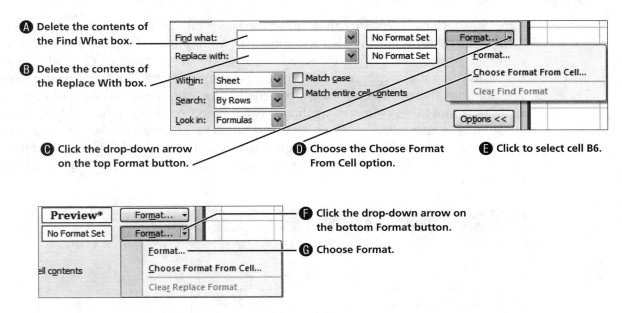

F Click the drop-down arrow on the bottom Format button.

G Choose Format.

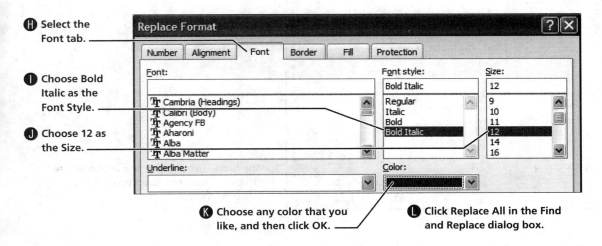

H Select the Font tab.

I Choose Bold Italic as the Font Style.

J Choose 12 as the Size.

K Choose any color that you like, and then click OK.

L Click Replace All in the Find and Replace dialog box.

6. Click OK, and then click Close to close the Find and Replace dialog box.

Using AutoCorrect

Excel's AutoCorrect feature can improve the speed and accuracy of entering text. AutoCorrect is most useful for replacing abbreviations with a full phrase of up to 255 characters. For example, you could set up AutoCorrect to substitute *Mr. Fitzpatrick's Class* whenever you type *mfc*. AutoCorrect also automatically corrects common misspellings and typographical errors. For example, the word *the* is often misspelled as *teh*, and the word *and* is often misspelled as *adn*. These and other common spelling mistakes are fixed automatically. AutoCorrect also automatically capitalizes the first letter of a day if you type it in lowercase. For example, if you type *sunday* and complete the entry, AutoCorrect will enter *Sunday* in the cell. Finally, AutoCorrect fixes words that have two initial capital letters by switching the second letter to lowercase.

The AutoCorrect dialog box allows you to customize how the AutoCorrect feature will work for you.

Expanding AutoCorrect Entries

AutoCorrect goes into action when you type a word in a text entry and tap Spacebar or when you complete a text entry. The word or entry is compared with all entries in the AutoCorrect table. The AutoCorrect table contains a list of words and their replacement phrases. If the word you type matches an entry in the AutoCorrect table, a phrase from the table is substituted for the word. This is known as expanding the AutoCorrect entry.

Undoing AutoCorrect Entries

There may be times that AutoCorrect replaces an entry against your wishes. AutoCorrect is treated as a single "character," meaning that it is viewed by the Undo feature the same as if you typed an "a" or tapped Delete. Therefore, you can use the Undo feature you learned about in Lesson 2, Editing, Viewing, and Printing Worksheets, to reverse an AutoCorrect entry.

Creating and Editing AutoCorrect Entries

The AutoCorrect dialog box allows you to add entries to the AutoCorrect table, delete entries from the table, and set other AutoCorrect options. To add an entry, type the desired abbreviation in the Replace box and the desired expansion for the abbreviation in the With box.

 ## Hands-On 5.6   Use AutoCorrect

1. Select cell A1.

2. Type **teh cat adn dog ran fast**, and then tap Enter.

3. Click cell A1.

4. Type **adn** and tap Spacebar.

5. Use Ctrl+Z to undo the last command.

6. Tap Esc to cancel the entry.

7. Choose Office → Excel Options.

8. Follow these steps to display the AutoCorrect dialog box:

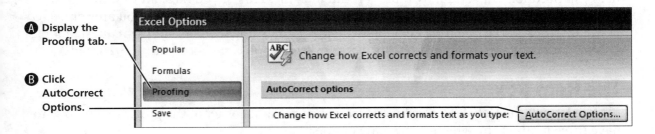

Ⓐ Display the Proofing tab.

Ⓑ Click AutoCorrect Options.

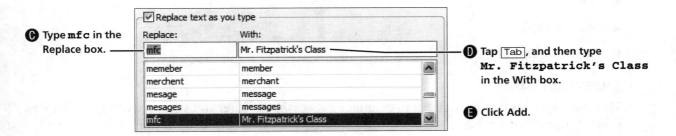

Ⓒ Type **mfc** in the Replace box.

Ⓓ Tap Tab, and then type **Mr. Fitzpatrick's Class** in the With box.

Ⓔ Click Add.

9. Click OK in the AutoCorrect dialog box.

10. Click OK in the Excel Options dialog box.

11. Ensure that cell A1 is still selected.

12. Type **mfc**, and then tap Enter.

13. Change the font size of cell A1 to 24.

14. Choose Office → Excel Options.

15. Display the Proofing tab.

16. Click AutoCorrect Options.

17. Follow these steps to delete the AutoCorrect entry you have created:

Ⓐ Type mfc in the Replace box.

Ⓑ Click Delete, and then tap [Enter].

Ⓒ Click OK.

18. Use [Ctrl] + [S] to save your work.

Using Excel's Help Feature

Excel's online Help feature puts a complete reference book at your fingertips. You can get the help you need for just about any topic you can imagine. Plus, if you have an Internet connection, additional help is available directly from the Microsoft website. When you are connected to the Internet and search for a help topic, Help automatically searches for the requested topics at Microsoft.com and displays a results list from which you can choose the desired topic.

The Help Box

You launch the Help box via a button near the top-right corner of the program window. You have three methods by which to navigate online help:

- Question Box

- Browse Topics

- Table of Contents

Question Box

This method uses powerful natural-language processing to interpret your question and display several items that are likely to contain the answer. Simply type your question in the box and tap [Enter]. The Help box displays a list of items related to your question.

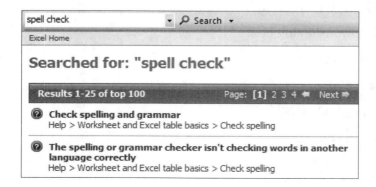

Browse Help

Categorized lists display commonly performed tasks. Each category features a list of subcategories and individual items that give instructions to perform specific tasks.

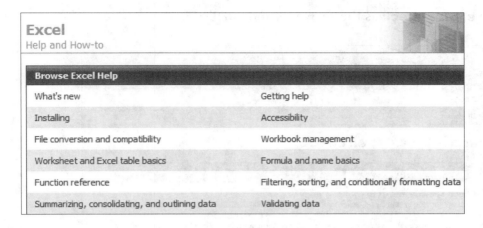

Search the Table of Contents

The Table of Contents panel displays the complete online help content in a hierarchical format that you can expand and collapse. Browsing the table of contents can often be a good way to search when you're not quite certain of a feature's name.

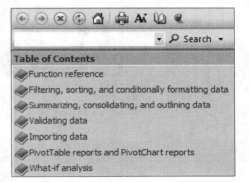

Finding Help When You Need It

In order to access Help in Excel 2007, you will need to click on the Help button to the far right of the Ribbon tabs. In addition, you can tap the F1 key to search Help.

The Help Window Toolbar

The toolbar in the Excel Help window looks very similar to the toolbar seen in Internet Explorer. It allows you to navigate Excel's help topics much the same way as you navigate through the Internet.

FROM THE KEYBOARD

F1 to find help

The buttons on the Help window toolbar look very similar to buttons you may be used to seeing on your Internet browser.

Hands-On 5.7   Use Help

1. Click the Help ⓐ button.

2. Type **spell check** as the keywords and tap [Enter].

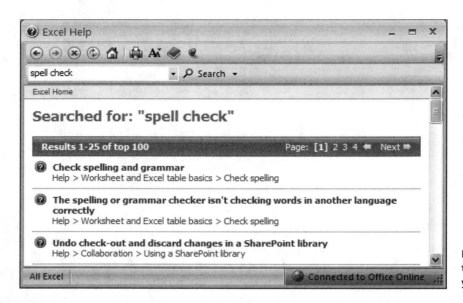

Excel will display all of the results relating to your keyword search.

3. Click the result titled "Check spelling and grammar."

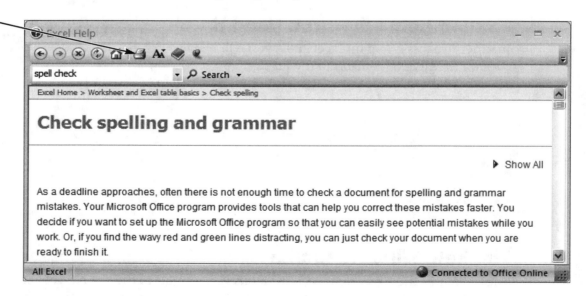

4. Think of a task that you would like to be able to perform in Excel.

5. Use Excel's Help window to search for instructions on how to complete the task.

6. Close the Excel Help window.

Using Excel's Proofing Tools

Excel comes with powerful proofing tools to aid you in your work. These tools appear in the Proofing group on the Review tab of the Ribbon.

The Proofing group on the Review tab of the Ribbon

Spelling Checker

Excel's spelling checker helps you to locate spelling errors in your worksheet. The Spelling feature checks the spelling of all text entries in the current worksheet. Excel's spelling checker functions much like the one in Microsoft Word, with which it shares the same main and custom dictionaries. The following Quick Reference table describes the options available.

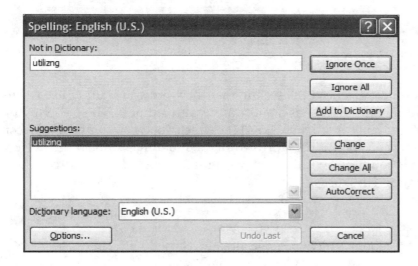

When you issue the spelling checker command, Excel will display the Spelling box that allows you to choose how to deal with words not in the dictionary.

Research References

Excel's Research task pane gives access to various useful reference sources and research sites. Most of this information arrives via an Internet connection. The following are examples of these resources:

- Dictionary and thesaurus
- Encyclopedia
- Stock quote services

Research Options

Choosing the Research Options button at the bottom of the Research pane displays a dialog box of research sources that Excel will search for answers to your queries. The categories from which you may choose are Reference Books, Research Sites, Business and Financial Sites, and Other Services.

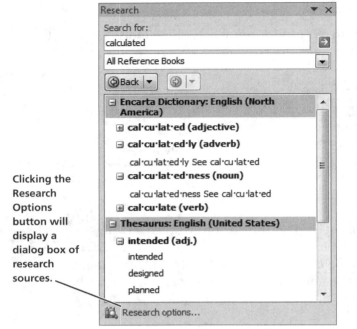

Clicking the Research Options button will display a dialog box of research sources.

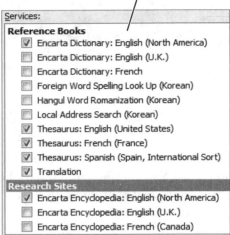

Research services, "books," and websites are displayed in the dialog box.

The Research Options button displays various reference and research sources.

Thesaurus

Have you ever experienced the feeling that the word you want to use is "just on the tip of your tongue"? Excel has a built-in thesaurus that can help you to find just that right word. If a cell contains the word for which you wish to find a replacement, simply click on it and then choose Thesaurus from the Proofing group on the Review tab of the Ribbon. If the word is contained within a cell with multiple words, double-click the word to select it before choosing Thesaurus.

Translation

In addition to the tools about which we have already learned, Excel also provides a tool that allows you to translate words and phrases into another language. The figure at right shows the languages into which you can translate your English word or phrase.

Hands-On 5.8   Work with Proofing Tools

1. Choose Review→Proofing→Spelling 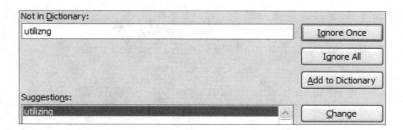 from the Ribbon.

2. Click the Change button to accept the suggested spelling.

3. Continue with the spelling check, accepting the suggestions for the last four misspellings.

4. Click OK to close the window indicating that the spelling check is complete for the entire sheet.

5. Use [Ctrl]+[S] to save your work.

6. Select cell F4.

7. Choose Review→Proofing→Research from the Ribbon.

8. Click the Start Searching button on the Research pane.

9. Choose Review→Proofing→Research from the Ribbon to close the Research pane.

10. Scroll down and select cell B24.

11. Double-click the word *understand* in the Formula Bar.

12. Choose Review→Proofing→Thesaurus from the Ribbon.

13. Tap [Enter] to close the cell for editing and issue the search command.

14. Select cell A2.

15. Choose Review→Proofing→Translate from the Ribbon.

16. Choose Italian as the language to which to translate.

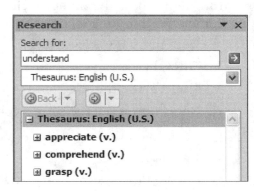

17. Take a look at the translation in the Research pane, and then Close [X] the task pane.

18. Use [Ctrl]+[S] to save your file.

19. Close [X] the Excel window.

Concepts Review

True/False Questions

1. After you rotate text within a cell, you must manually resize the row to fit the rotated text.   TRUE   FALSE

2. The AutoFit command changes the column width to fit the narrowest entry in the column.   TRUE   FALSE

3. Row heights cannot be adjusted using AutoFit.   TRUE   FALSE

4. New columns are inserted to the left of selected columns.   TRUE   FALSE

5. Using the Research task pane, you can download current stock quotes from the Internet.   TRUE   FALSE

6. Hidden columns and rows will not print.   TRUE   FALSE

7. Excel's Spelling tool shares its dictionary with Word and other Office applications.   TRUE   FALSE

8. You can search Excel Help by using keywords.   TRUE   FALSE

9. You must program an AutoCorrect entry in each Office application in which you wish to use it.   TRUE   FALSE

10. You can find and replace cell formatting as well as text entries.   TRUE   FALSE

Multiple Choice Questions

1. How many rows are inserted if you select three rows and choose the Home→Cells→Insert command from the Ribbon?
   a. One, above the selection
   b. Three, below the selection
   c. Three, above the selection
   d. None; that is not the correct command

2. How can you reverse an AutoCorrect entry?
   a. Tap ⟨Delete⟩
   b. Choose Edit→Reverse→Undo from the Ribbon
   c. Click the Undo button on the Quick Access toolbar
   d. Tap ⟨Backspace⟩

3. Which of the following is not a method by which you can search for help in Excel?
   a. Indexed Topic List
   b. Browse Help Topics
   c. Table of Contents
   d. Question Box

4. Which Excel tool would you use to help you find just the right word?
   a. Encyclopedia
   b. Thesaurus
   c. Translation
   d. Research

Index

L

line breaks, 61
Live Preview, 57–58

M

margins, page, 10, 34
Maximum function, 40
Merge and Center option, 61, 62
merging/splitting cells, 60–62
Minimum function, 40
Mini toolbar, 57–58
mixed cell references, 44
mouse, navigating with, 5

N

negative numbers, 13, 64
NOW( ) function, 71
Number Command group, 63
numbers, formatting, 13–14,
    63–65

O

Office button, 8
operators, arithmetic, 42–43

P

Page Layout view, 10–11, 33–34
pages, formatting, 10, 34
paste functions, 25–28, 47–49
percent number format, 63, 64
point mode, 44, 45
printing, 34–36
Print Preview feature, 34, 36
proofreading tools, 91

Q

Quick Access toolbar, 8–9, 10

R

ranges of cells, 23–25
Redo and Undo buttons, 28
references, cell, 42–43, 44–46
relative cell references, 44
replacing objects, 83–85
Research task pane, 91
Ribbon, 8–10, 57–58
right-dragging technique, 26

rotating objects, text in Excel
    cells, 81–83
rows and columns, 75–81

S

Save As command, 15
ScreenTips, 9
scrolling in worksheets, 5, 6
searching cell contents, 83–85
selection methods, cells, 5, 23–25
shading and borders, 66–68
sheet tabs in worksheets, 4, 5
shift cells option, 77
Shrink to Fit option, 61, 62
spell checking, 91
splitting/merging cells, 60–62
spreadsheets
    (*see also* cells)
    deleting data, 22
    editing entries, 11, 21–22,
        25–30
    entering data, 11–13
    opening, 21
    printing, 35–36
    saving, 15–16
status bar, 4, 40
styles, numbers, 63
Sum function, 39–41

T

tabs
    Excel window, 8–9
    sheet tabs in worksheets, 4, 5
text
    indenting, 59–60
    line breaks, 61
    long entries in Excel, 11
    rotating in cells, 81–83
    wrapping within cells, 61–62
themes, 69–70
thesaurus tool, 92–93
time functions, 71
TODAY( ) function, 71
translation tool, 92

U

Undo and Redo buttons, 28–29

V

vertical alignment in cells, 81, 82

W

what-if analyses, 45
workbooks/worksheets
    closing, 17
    definition, 5
    navigating in, 5, 6
    opening, 21
    saving, 15–17
    sheet tabs, 4, 5
wrapping text option, 61–62

Z

Zoom feature, 4, 33, 33–34